'*The Low Allergy Garden* by Mark Ragg will be welcomed by the many thousands and thousands of people who suffer every year from seasonal hayfever, asthma and skin allergies. It tells them in an easy-to-read style how to reduce symptoms by establishing a low allergy garden – describing each plant, listing both popular and botanical names, and whether they may cause problems for people with allergies. The Asthma Foundation of NSW first realised the need to increase public awareness of low allergen gardening by producing an information leaflet and creating a low allergen garden display at the Royal Botanical Gardens, Sydney, both of which generated an unprecedented level of public interest. We believe this book will be of great benefit for people with springtime asthma and allergies.'

MRS JUNE HAYES, Vice President, Asthma Foundation of NSW

'This book will be of wide use to people who have an interest in health and the environment for it provides a wealth of information about how plants can affect us if we are unfortunate enough to become sensitised to them. In Australia and New Zealand there are many allergenic plants to be found in gardens, city plantings and waste ground. The useful compilations given in the book illustrate the range of plants which may affect us – whether by inhalation of pollen or fragments from pollen grains, or by contact of plants with the skin. The book also provides a very readable account of our understanding of allergens from both the plant perspective, as well as our own following the contact of pollen with our lung surfaces. Pollen arrives from both local and more distant sources. *The Low Allergy Garden* provides much useful information to reduce local effects by identifying problem plant species which produce allergenic pollen or contact irritants.'

D. W. FOUNTAIN, Associate Professor of Plant Biology, Department of Plant Biology and Biotechnology, Massey University, Palmerston North, New Zealand

'Dr Mark Ragg deserves all our congratulations for writing such an excellent book – it is always hard to write the 'first', and this book is extraordinarily comprehensive and helpful to the Australasian gardener. It gives us all a new and comprehensive picture of allergic diseases – hayfever, asthma and skin complaints that are triggered by the reaction of our immune system to factors in our environment, especially plants in the garden. The incidence of allergic diseases has never been higher, particularly among children in Australia and New Zealand. It is good to read in this book of the practical things that we can do ourselves to significantly improve our outdoor environment and reduce the incidence of asthma and allergies. It is a source of user-friendly and interesting information on allergic diseases, and how and why we become sensitised to plants. This book is a must for gardeners who have experienced skin rashes and other allergies after gardening. There are several books that tell us what not to plant in our gardens, but this book is unique in advising us what we *should* plant!'

DR R. BRUCE KNOX DSC, PHD, FAA
Professor of Botany
The University of Melbourne

GARDENS FOR PEOPLE
WITH ASTHMA AND ALLERGIES

# THE LOW ALLERGY

[ G A R D E N ]

*Gardens you can enjoy without*
*sneezing, wheezing, itching, watery eyes*
*or runny noses*

## MARK RAGG

*Illustrations by Frances Bodkin*

Hodder & Stoughton

A Hodder & Stoughton Book

Published in Australia and New Zealand in 1996 by
Hodder Headline Australia Pty Limited
(A member of the Hodder Headline Group)
10-16 South Street, Rydalmere NSW 2116

Reprinted 1998

**National Library of Australia Cataloguing-in-Publication data**

Ragg, Mark.
The low allergy garden: gardens you can enjoy without
sneezing, wheezing, itching, watery eyes or runny noses.

Includes index.
ISBN 0 7336 0265 7.

1. Gardening – Therapeutic use. 2. Allergy – Popular works.
3. Asthma – Popular works. 4. Hay fever plants. I. Title.

616.97

Cover design by Vivien Valk
Printed in Australia by Griffin Press Pty Ltd, Netley, South Australia

# Thanks

There's only one name on the cover, but *The Low Allergy Garden* has not been a solo effort. It has been a collaborative effort between a group of skilled and knowledgeable people, and an author grateful for all the wisdom thrown at him.

Primarily, I would like to thank Diana Bass, an allergist with a special interest in gardens, who has spent many years carrying out the painstaking research that forms the basis of this book. She has spent twenty years, apart from her other duties as a visiting medical officer at Concord Hospital in Sydney, collecting pollens, describing them and analysing them. She also searched through the medical literature, history books and archives to put together Australia's only national pollen calendar, which we have reproduced with her permission in Chapter 6.

Diana wrote a remarkably popular brochure on low allergen gardens for the Asthma Foundation of New South Wales, which sparked our interest in writing a book about it. If she had had the time to get away from her research, she would have written this book herself.

I would also like to thank Peter Thorburn, director of Honeysuckle Garden in Sydney. Peter is a nurseryman who has asthma, and he has turned his combined talents to good use. Our conversations enabled me to work out how to turn a list of plants into a useful book. Much of the practical knowledge in this book is his.

Frances Bodkin's assistance has been tremendous. Firstly, she wrote *Encyclopaedia Botanica*, a useful reference of plants found in Australia and available in Australian nurseries which has formed the basis of my descriptions of the characteristics of plants. As well, apart from providing dinner to a stranger at short notice when I called seeking information, she supplied me with several chapters from her forthcoming book on dangerous plants, without a qualm that publication by somebody else would pre-empt her. This information has formed the basis of Chapter 16.

I also received valuable advice and comments on a first draft of this book from June Hayes, vice president of the Asthma Foundation of New South Wales; Margo Lemcke, education officer at the same organisation; Ian Innes, horticultural development officer with the Royal Botanic Gardens,

Sydney; Margaret Hanks, the Royal Botanic Garden's garden advisory service officer; Bruce Knox, professor of botany at the University of Melbourne; and keen amateur gardeners Sonja Bryson and Wal Ragg.

Moreen Woollett of the Society for Growing Australian Plants, Graeme Greenhalgh of Tropic of Sydney and Susanne Freeman, a dermatologist of note, also provided much-needed help.

Finally, I would like to thank Philippa Sandall for her inspiration, guidance and considerable skills.

MARK RAGG

*Viola x wittrochiana cultivars (pansy)*

# CONTENTS

## Part I
## ALLERGIES

## Part II
## PLANTS TO CHOOSE FOR
## YOUR LOW ALLERGY GARDEN

## Part III
# PLANTS TO AVOID

## Part IV
# GOOD GARDENING

# INTRODUCTION

If the Australasian dream is to own your home, then part of that dream lies with having a garden. Whether it's a few square metres of paving behind a terrace, an 800 square metre suburban block, two hectares on the outskirts of the city or the home paddocks on a sheep farm, we all like a bit of greenery around.

Gardens relax us. We sit in them and think. We watch them change with the seasons, whether subtlely or suddenly.

We use gardens to house our pets, our children and our hobbies. We get to mow our lawns, dig our gardens and cut them back. We can work all day in the garden, usually without thinking of it as work.

We use gardens to chase our children around, as refuges where we can slow down and actually talk to husbands, wives and lovers; and as home gymnasiums where we can exercise without the need for leotards.

Unfortunately, gardens are not kind to some people. Some of us are allergic to certain plants. Some of us find our hayfever worsens when we go outside, our asthma flares up or our skin erupts. Some of us feel shocking at certain times of the year. We itch, sneeze, wheeze, bark and scratch.

The aim of *The Low Allergy Garden* – to my knowledge the first such book in the world – is to provide information to people with allergies or allergy-based illnesses such as asthma, hayfever and dermatitis. It describes how to enjoy our gardens without wheezing, sneezing, itching or feeling burdened by ill health.

While doing the research for this book, I wondered whether it would be possible to have a low allergy garden and still have an interesting garden. Would a low allergy garden be too restricted?

That concern was satisfied by a wise garden designer, who pointed out that all gardens have limitations and constraints. For some, the constraints are the budget. For others, it's size. For others, it's the aspect, or the lack of rain, or the slope of the ground. If you want a good garden, you can have one – low allergy or not.

Part I of this book deals with allergies - what causes them, their role in asthma, hayfever and skin rashes, and the role of plants in causing allergies. It also provides pollen calendars for Australia and New Zealand, to give some guidance as to which pollens are around at what times of the year.

Part II goes into the plants. Chapters 7 to 13 provide page after page of plants that have been tested scientifically and found not to worsen asthma and hayfever.

Part III lists plants to avoid, in three separate chapters. Chapter 14 lists those plants which have been proved to worsen asthma or hayfever in susceptible people. Chapter 15 lists those plants which might cause contact dermatitis. Chapter 16 lists those plants which might give skin rashes if you touch them.

You may notice that there are a few plants which make it into two lists. This is because some plants have been tested and found to produce little or no allergenic pollen, but they can still irritate the skin if touched. Rather than rule them out altogether, they have been included where required. You, as the gardener, can decide whether it is possible to avoid touching an irritant but low allergen plant.

Part IV provides information on how to garden effectively without worsening your allergies, and includes a series of logical and easy-to-follow tips on sensible low allergy gardening.

When you get to the middle section, you will see that I have used two names for plants – the common name in plain type and the botanical name in italics. There are two reasons for this.

One is that a few people are very snooty about plants, and don't believe that a *Rosa* would smell as sweet by any other name. The botanical names keep them happy.

The main reason, however, is that common names can be misleading, especially when you are trying to decide which plants may harm your health.

For example, in Chapter 11 we write about rosemary, a common enough plant, and give the botanical name *Rosmarinus officinalis*. This is to make it clear which one we are talking about, because there are a few other plants named rosemary, including bog rosemary (*Andromeda polifolia*), marsh rosemary (*Statice caroliniana*), coastal rosemary (*Westringia fruticosa*), native rosemary (*Westringia* spp.) and wild Rosemary (*Ledum palustre*). Note that four different genera are mentioned, and none of them is the same as the plant that we know as rosemary.

The importance of this is that those other species have not been tested rigorously in the way that *Rosmarinus officinalis* has, so it is the only one we can say is safe for people with allergies. The other species, which we also know as rosemaries, may well be dangerous, or they may not. We just don't know.

On top of that, many plants have different common names in different states, cities, and even in different suburbs. So if you're going to use this book as a guide for buying plants for your garden, you need the botanical name to ensure you have the right one. We have given the botanical name first and cross-referenced with the common names as much as possible.

There are something like two million people with asthma in Australia and New Zealand, and a similar number of people have hayfever. It's hard to know what proportion of that huge group find their allergies worsened by a garden. We hope every single one of them has an opportunity to read this book and find it helpful.

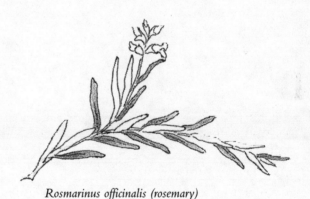

*Rosmarinus officinalis (rosemary)*

# Part I
# ALLERGIES

What is Allergy? • Asthma • Other Allergic

Conditions • Pollen and Other Allergies

• Assessing Allergies • The Pollen Season

# CHAPTER 1
# WHAT IS ALLERGY?

Allergy is a reaction of the body to a stimulus that it doesn't like. It might be a swelling, an itch, a rash, a wheeze or even a cough.

While the most obvious allergies are the blatant ones that occur when you eat a peanut and break out in hives, or use a new detergent and get a rash where the clothes touch your skin, allergies play a part in other illnesses.

The main ones of concern to gardeners are asthma and hayfever. Some people might think it odd to hear asthma described as an allergy-based illness but, for some people, it is.

Perhaps 20 per cent of people with asthma find they are wheezier during certain times of the year, or when the wind is up, or when they go outside. There are quite a few asthmatics who can't mow the lawn without a puffer in their hand. Not everybody with asthma is affected by allergies, but there are enough who are to make it well worth considering.

There are a thousand other diseases in which the immune system plays a part, and some of them are listed in the table on page 4. It is impossible to know whether or not plant allergies and pollens play a part in these diseases, as the research required to answer those questions has not been done.

## The immune system

Allergic reactions occur because the immune system reacts to something it doesn't like. But what is the immune system?

The immune system is a large and complex part of the body's defences against the outside world. It has many, many different functions. The main ones are that it:

* attacks bacteria, viruses and other invaders;
* plays a part in preventing cancers;

- helps repair cut skin and broken bones; and
- preserves us as individuals.

The immune system is not one simple organ, like a heart or a kidney, but a range of tissues and cells scattered around the body. It comprises a range of different blood cells and a few collections of specialised tissue which is known as lymphoid tissue. The lymphoid tissue includes the following.

**The thymus,** which is a small gland at the top of the chest whose main role is to produce T-cells.

**Lymph nodes,** also known as glands, which collect some of the blood's waste.

**The spleen,** which is an organ under the ribs on the left whose main role is to collect and break down decaying red blood cells.

**The tonsils,** adenoids and the appendix are also mainly lymphoid tissue.

There are many different types of cells in the immune system. The main ones are lymphocytes (which can be either T-cells or B-cells), plasma cells and macrophages. For the sake of a low allergy garden, the most important cells are the B-cells.

B-cells are produced in the bone marrow and released into the blood, where they drift around looking for something to do. When a B-cell spots something that shouldn't be in the blood, like a virus, then it wanders over and makes itself known. When it meets the virus, or any other invader, the B-cell measures it up. It takes a good look at the virus, and starts the process of producing antibodies, which are long chains of protein. These antibodies, when released, will go and attack that virus, attempting to kill it. Antibodies usually succeed.

The first time your immune system meets an invader, whether it be a virus, a bacterium or anything else, it takes up to ten days or so to produce the antibody to do the job. The next time that virus gets into your bloodstream, the antibodies are ready to go, and can be released within hours.

# Allergy

Allergies occur when your immune system produces antibodies to battle things that it should not battle. For example, if you are allergic to seafood, then every time you eat seafood, the immune system recognises cells from the fish and starts producing antibodies.

---

**Allergy is the body's way of saying:**
**'We've met before, and once is enough.'**

---

If you tend to be allergic to quite a few different things, or if you suffer asthma and hayfever and get dermatitis, you are an atopic person. Atopy is a hereditary disposition to develop allergies.

---

### ILLNESSES IN WHICH A MALFUNCTION OF THE IMMUNE SYSTEM PLAYS A PART

| | |
|---|---|
| Anaemia (some types) | Leprosy |
| Asthma | Lymphoma |
| Cancer | Rheumatoid arthritis |
| Eczema | Systemic lupus erythematosus (SLE) |
| Glomerulonephritis | Thyroid disease (some types) |
| Hayfever | Ulcerative colitis |
| Hepatitis (some types) | Urticaria |
| Hodgkin's disease | |

---

## ALLERGY: A MODERN CONCEPT

The concept of allergy is a modern one. The word 'allergy' doesn't rate a mention in the body of my edition of the *Shorter Oxford English Dictionary*, which is based on the first *Oxford English Dictionary*, which was developed in the latter half of the nineteenth century. It appears only in the Addenda, surrounded by other more modern words and usages as algorithm, alibi, alienation, alley-way and allure.

The word appears to have been coined by a German pathologist named von Pirquet in 1906, who combined two Greek words, one meaning 'other' or 'different' and the other as part of the word 'energy'. By 1911, pathologists were using the word in English.

So if the concept of allergy existed before 1906, it was very different from the way we think of the word.

# CHAPTER 2
# ASTHMA

Asthma is a disorder of breathing which affects about 20 per cent of children, 15 per cent of teenagers and 10 per cent of adults in Australia and New Zealand. Those figures stand true for city, suburbs, bush, beach and mountains. It seems to be getting more common and more severe in children.

Many years ago, asthma was quite a dangerous illness because there were few effective treatments. Now, it is simple to manage for most people. It can still be dangerous, but mainly because some people either don't know about effective treatments, or because they don't stick to the treatments they have been prescribed. Also, there are a few people whose asthma is quite unpredictable and difficult to control.

**Most people who have asthma lead normal, productive lives with few worries.**

## Normal breathing

We usually breathe in and out twelve to fifteen times a minute, or something close to 20 000 times a day. Each time we breathe, about 500 millilitres of air goes in. That gives a total of about 10 000 litres of air going in and out each day.

Each time we breathe, air comes in through the nose and/or mouth. The nose is the organ actually designed for breathing – it has hairs to filter out impurities and a narrowed passage to ensure the air is warmed and humidified as it passes through. The air then passes into the pharynx at the back of the throat, then into the trachea, bronchi and lungs.

All the way through, the airways are covered with a smooth lining. This lining is similar to that lining your mouth – smooth and moist.

Outside the lining, the airways have a layer of muscle. This muscle is not under voluntary control, like the muscles in your legs, but is controlled by the brain without your conscious input. These muscles contract and relax, but you can't make them do it.

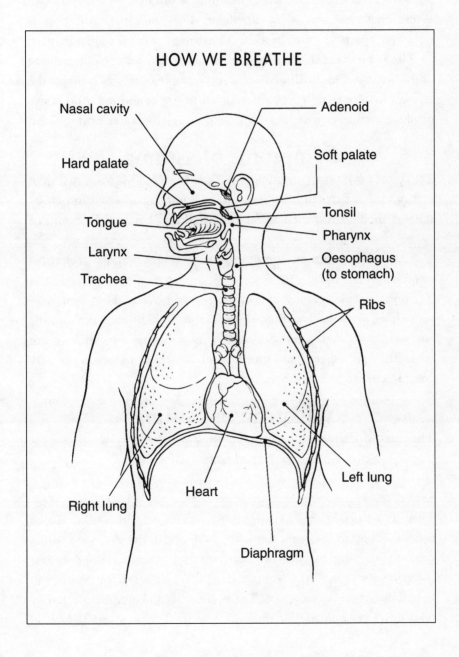

## HOW WE BREATHE

Nasal cavity

Adenoid

Hard palate

Soft palate

Tongue

Tonsil

Larynx

Pharynx

Trachea

Oesophagus (to stomach)

Ribs

Left lung

Right lung

Heart

Diaphragm

# What goes wrong?

We used to think of asthma as being mainly a constriction of the muscles around the airways. It was thought that if you could relieve the muscle constriction, then breathing would be easier. Now, we realise that this was a bit simplistic. The muscle constriction is definitely part of the problem, but it is not the major part.

The main event that causes asthma is an inflammation of the lining of the airways. This inflammation does a couple of things. It makes the airways smaller, making it harder for air to get in and out. And it also produces mucus, which makes you cough and feel off colour.

# Symptoms of asthma

The most common symptom of asthma is a cough. It is a dry, tight sort of cough that tends to be worse at night, and is eased in part by reliever medications such as Ventolin, Bricanyl, Respax, Respolin or Asmol.

The other common symptoms are a wheeze and a feeling of tightness in the chest.

Some people get other symptoms. Some feel like they have something at the back of their throat. Some feel like they can't handle any weight on their chest. Some develop a foul taste in their mouth when they are wheezy and producing mucus. But the main ones are cough, wheeze and tightness.

# What causes asthma?

There is no simple explanation of what goes wrong in asthma, but there are a number of interrelated factors.

## Genetics

There is no doubt that a tendency to asthma runs in families. To be more precise, atopy begets atopy. For example, in my extended family I have asthmatic parents, brothers, sisters, cousins and about four thousand (or so it seems) asthmatic nephews. If I had any nieces, I'm sure they'd have asthma, too. There are a few people in my family who don't get asthma, but they get eczema. There's also a fair bit of chronic hayfever, and some of us are prone to urticaria. We are an atopic family. There are many like us.

## Early exposure to allergens

Some evidence has emerged recently that babies who live in dusty houses and sleep in dusty rooms are more likely to develop asthma than those who live and sleep in clean rooms and houses.

The problem is not the dust itself, but a small creature known as the house dust mite. This animal lives where dust gathers, and its faeces are highly allergenic. House dust mites thrive in warm, humid environments and tend to be found in high concentrations in bedding and in carpets.

Dusty houses in the first year of life don't cause asthma, but they make it more likely that asthma will develop in a child who is genetically susceptible. Genetically susceptible children who are not exposed to house dust mites may not develop asthma.

## Triggers

There are many many things that can spark off an attack of asthma in someone who is genetically susceptible. Most people with asthma will find that some of these triggers will not affect them, while others quickly induce wheeziness.

The main potential triggers are:
• viral infections, such as a cold;
• allergens, such as pollen, mould, house dust mite
  and animal dander;
• exercise;
• cold air.

Other potential triggers include:
• a change in the weather;
• chemical sensitivities;
• aspirin;
• anti-inflammatory medications such as Naprosyn, Indocid, Orudis
  and others;

- beta-blockers, which are drugs used to treat heart disease, high blood pressure and glaucoma;
- some foods and food additives;
- stress and high emotion;
- some strong smells such as perfume, plant perfumes and paint fumes;
- thunderstorms;
- cigarette smoke;
- some workplaces with industrial chemicals, wood dust and flour;
- sulphur oxides, which are emitted by kerosene heaters and the burning of fossil fuels;
- industrial pollution, particular diesel fumes.

Chapter 18 will discuss how to deal with some of these precipitants.

# Dealing with asthma

There are four main ways to manage your asthma. These are:
- preventing asthma;
- avoiding triggers;
- treating symptoms;
- understanding your asthma.

## *Preventing asthma*

There is a whole range of medications that prevent asthma attacks, or at least make the attacks less severe when they do occur. The most commonly used preventive medications are Intal, Tilade, Vicrom (available in New Zealand), and corticosteroids. Corticosteroids can be either inhaled (as Becotide, Becloforte, Aldecin, Pulmicort, Respocort and Flixotide) or taken as tablets (as prednisone).

These medications dampen down the immune system in the lining of the lungs, so that the lungs don't respond to whatever usually makes them react. So if you normally get asthma when you get a cold, taking a preventive medication won't stop the cold, but it may prevent the asthma that often goes with it.

These medications must be taken every day, or they don't work. If you stop and start them, they can't do their job.

Also, they all become more effective with time. They may not even start to work for a few days, and you may not get much benefit from them for a week or two. They are still continuing to improve for months. So if you start them, you need to persevere.

## STEROIDS

The steroids used to prevent or treat asthma are not the same ones sold on the black market for gym junkies. If inhaled at the recommended doses, they are unlikely to produce side effects on the rest of the body. Their effects are restricted to the lungs.

## *Avoiding triggers*

That, really, is what this book is about. Something like half of all asthmatics who have a skin prick allergy test will find that they are allergic to grasses or pollens or something in the garden. And about half of that group, when they really think about it, will find that their symptoms do occur at certain times of the year, or in certain conditions (such as during thunderstorms, or on hot windy days).

*It is this group of people who may benefit from designing and building a low allergy garden.*

Then there are other triggers to avoid. See Chapter 18 for more details on how to avoid precipitants.

## *Treating symptoms*

If you have asthma, you will know that no matter what you do, you are going to get it at some time. If you take preventive treatments and avoid precipitants, your asthma will come on less often and will be less severe when it happens, but it is still going to happen.

That is when you need Ventolin or one of the similar products such as Respolin, Respax or Asmol, which are versions of the drug salbutamol, or Bricanyl, which is a version of terbutaline. They are all known as relieving medications or bronchodilators.

Relieving medications work by relaxing the muscles around your airways, allowing them to open up. This allows you to breathe more easily. Even though they only work for a few hours, and even though they do nothing to deal with the inflammation that is the real problem with asthma, relievers are very good short term treatments for asthma.

Most people know of the Ventolin puffer. If you have asthma, you should have a puffer with you at all times.

It would also be worth getting something known as a spacer device, which is a hollow clear plastic tube. The adult spacer looks something like a football. Spacers have a hole in one end, into which the puffer fits. They have a mouthpiece and valve on the other end. You puff the medication into the spacer, then slowly breathe it in through the valve.

Spacers are effective in two ways. They get rid of the problem of trying to coordinate the puff with the breath. And they also deliver more medication to the lungs than does the puffer alone.

The other essential device for some asthmatics is the nebuliser. This is a pump with a hose and mask attachment. You put liquid medication in a bowl attached to the mask and turn the nebuliser on. The medication is turned into a fine mist, which you breathe in.

But consider this. If you are needing relieving medication every day, or even three times a week, your asthma is not under good control. You should see your doctor – you probably should be taking preventive medication every day as well.

# CHECK YOUR PUFFERS

One common trap is that puffers can either run out, or go out of date, without you realising it. You should always check the date on your puffers and other medications, and replace them if past the expiry date.

Also, you should check that your puffers actually contain medication. You can do this by taking the puffer out of its container and floating it in water. If it sinks, it is full. If it sits high in the water, it might be empty. The diagram gives examples.

## MEASURING HOW MUCH
## MEDICATION IS LEFT

The illustration shows a simple method for checking the amount of medication in the canister.

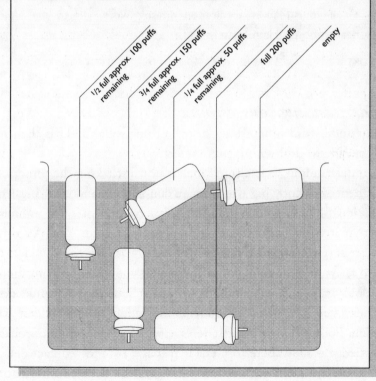

## WHEN TO SEEK HELP

One of the hardest things about asthma is to know when to seek help. Here's a basic plan.

• If you have increased your medication, or if you are waking at night with asthma, or if you are wheezy first thing in the morning, or if you can't exercise without coughing, you should see your family doctor within twenty-four hours.

• If you are taking your relieving medication every three hours, you should see your family doctor within a few hours.

• If you are taking your relieving medication every two hours, you should either see your doctor or go to the emergency department of your nearest hospital immediately.

• If you are taking your relieving medication every hour, you should get to an emergency department immediately. Either call an ambulance, or ask someone to drive you there.

• If your reliever medication doesn't work, get to the nearest hospital immediately.

## *Understanding your asthma*

If you understand your asthma, or the asthma your child has, then you will be able to deal with it more effectively.

Understanding your asthma means not just taking the prescribed treatments, but knowing why you are taking them and knowing what does what. It means understanding what triggers off your asthma – whether it be exercise or foods or lawns or a cold – and knowing how its severity can be reduced.

So apart from noticing what goes on in your own life, you should seek out as much information as you can. Some doctors and nurses are very good at providing information, while others are not. The Asthma Foundation in your state or city is a good source of reliable knowledge – see Where to Get Help (page 143) for contact details. And there are plenty of books which give the detailed information you need to really understand asthma.

As well, understanding your asthma means monitoring it. It can be very difficult, when you have asthma, to really perceive how bad it is. Objective measures such as a peak flow metre can help you monitor your asthma – see Chapter 18 for details.

Something like eight hundred Australians and one hundred and thirty New Zealanders a year die of asthma. One reason - not the only one, but it is an important one – is that some of them leave it too late to seek help.

---

**No doctor or nurse will laugh at you for overreacting
with asthma**

---

# CHAPTER 3
# OTHER ALLERGIC CONDITIONS

## Hayfever

Hayfever is common, affecting about 20 per cent of all Australians and New Zealanders. It affects people of all ages from babies to centenarians. It is most common in children and young adults. Although it is not terribly serious for most people, it is very annoying. And there are some people who suffer hayfever so badly that it interferes with their ability to lead a normal life.

Hayfever's most common symptoms are:
• sneezing;
• running nose;
• itchy eyes and nose;
• blocked nose.

Some people who have chronic hayfever also get frequent colds, recurrent headaches, a chronic cough and permanent tiredness. Some also develop sinusitis, which causes headaches and facial pain.

Children with hayfever may have permanently blocked noses, which leads them to breathe through their mouths, which leads to more respiratory infections. Mouth breathing also dries the airways, and this may make asthma even worse. Children with hayfever may also have trouble sleeping, making them tired and grumpy.

Hayfever is associated in some way with asthma, although the nature of the link is not clear. It tends to run in families, and it often runs in the same families as asthma.

# What causes hayfever?

Hayfever is triggered by allergies. Some people can define quite clearly that they develop hayfever when they get near a cat, or a wattle, or something else.

But many people who have hayfever don't know what induces it. That may be because they are allergic to so many things that it is hard to narrow down the trigger. Or it may be because they are allergic to something as common as grass or pollen, in which case it is hard to isolate the cause.

The most common causes of hayfever are:
• the house dust mite;
• grass pollens;
• cats.

However, almost anything can cause hayfever, including aspirin and certain foods.

# How is hayfever treated?

The best way to treat hayfever is to prevent it. You should try to avoid the triggers, if you can identify them. Chapter 18 will explain how this is done. There is a range of medications to treat hayfever.

**Decongestant sprays** will ease a blocked nose. These only work for short periods and tend to encourage reliance on them. They may damage the lining of the nose if used for prolonged periods. **Preventive sprays** such as Beconase, Rhinocort, Rynacrom, Rhinalar or Aldecin, which must be taken every day, will reduce the impact of allergies.

**Non-sedating antihistamine tablets** such as Teldane, Claratyne, Hismanal or Zyrtec will help stop the sneezing and runny nose.

---

**The best way to treat hayfever is to prevent it.**

---

## What are nasal polyps?

Nasal polyps are small benign growths inside the nose. They are probably caused by long term swelling of the lining of the nose, and may be associated with allergies.

Polyps can block the nose completely, making it impossible to breathe through one nostril – or both.

Treatment for polyps involves either long term steroid sprays (such as Beconase, Aldecin, Rhinalar or Rhinocort) to reduce the swelling (effective in most people within six weeks) or surgery to remove them. They may grow back, in which case you have the same treatment choices.

---

**What is seasonal allergic rhinitis?**
**Hayfever.**
**Seasonal allergic rhinitis is a term used by**
**people who like jargon.**

---

# Rashes

## Atopic dermatitis

Atopic dermatitis, or eczema, is a dry, scaly, itchy rash. It can appear anywhere on the body, although it is found most often on the face, eyebrows, trunk, back of the knees and folds of the elbows.

Many babies have eczema, and it becomes less common with age, often disappearing by the age of five. About 5 per cent of us have or have had eczema.

People with eczema may also have asthma and/or hayfever. These conditions may also be present in relatives.

Eczema may be worsened by:
• contact with allergens such as dust mites, animal fur, grass pollens and mould spores;
• food allergies, most commonly due to eggs, cow's milk, wheat, fish, soy and peanut products;
• stress;

- weather changes; or
- irritants such as woollen clothes, perfumes, soaps and chemicals.

Treatment involves avoiding whatever makes it worse, avoiding excessive drying of the skin and using appropriate creams.

## Contact dermatitis

Contact dermatitis is similar to atopic eczema, except that it occurs after you have come in contact with something. Plants aside, the most common culprits are:
- nickel, found in coins and stainless steel;
- chromium, found in cement and leather;
- rubber products in gloves and boots; and
- preservatives in creams, ointments and cosmetics.

Chapter 15 contains a comprehensive list of plants which are said to cause contact dermatitis. See that chapter for details.

## Hives (urticaria)

Hives are itchy red weals which can appear anywhere on the body at any time as an allergic response to … who knows what? Sometimes it is obvious that you got hives from contact with the rhus tree or a Robyn Gordon grevillea, for example, but often there is no obvious cause for the hives.

There are some plants, like those mentioned above, which are known to cause hives quite regularly. But almost anything can do it to you, if you are unlucky.

Antihistamine medications are the required treatment for hives. They usually fix the problem quite quickly.

*Grevillea 'Robyn Gordon'*

# CHAPTER 4
# POLLEN AND OTHER ALLERGENS

Plants reproduce by having flowers that give off pollen. The pollen is transported in one way or another to other similar plants, where it attaches to the stigma. There, the pollen swells and releases two sperm cells, which attach to the female egg of the recipient plant. If all goes well, the sperm fertilises the egg.

Plants distribute their pollen in two ways. One way is to produce small amounts of pollen that can be picked up by birds and insects. The birds and the bees carry the pollen from one plant to another, and deposit it where it does its stuff.

*Pollination by birds*

---

**What's the connection between gardens and allergies?
The main connection is pollen.**

---

The other way is for the plants to produce smaller, lighter pollen that can be carried by the breeze. It floats into the air, drifts on the currents and finally drops, hopefully onto the flower of a like-minded plant.

As you can imagine, the second method of pollination is fairly haphazard. Plants that rely on airborne pollination have to produce huge amounts of pollen in the hope that some lands in the right place.

It is these plants – those that rely on airborne pollination – that cause the problems for people with allergies. Their pollens are known as aeroallergens.

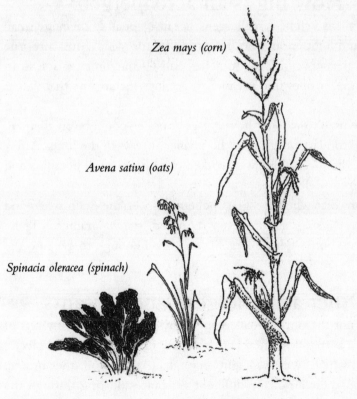

*Zea mays (corn)*

*Avena sativa (oats)*

*Spinacia oleracea (spinach)*

*Airborne pollination*

# What do aeroallergens do?

You could put it simply and say that an aeroallergen floats along, is breathed in and lodges in the lung, where it sets off an allergic reaction. While that is fairly close to the truth, things are not quite as simple as that.

Some allergens are too big to fit in the airway, yet still induce asthma. Other particles are the right size but, for some reason, do not provoke an allergic reaction.

Sometimes, the first explanation is the right one. But aeroallergens can affect you in other ways. For example, some particles landing in the nose stimulate a reflex that induces asthma. Other particles are absorbed into the bloodstream in the nose, mouth or throat, and cause their problems elsewhere in the body.

# How big is an aeroallergen?

Not all pollens will be aeroallergens, because not all of them are small enough and light enough to be carried by the wind. Most airborne allergens are between 2 micrometres and 60 micrometres across. In general, smaller ones find it easier to get into the airways than larger ones.

People used to wonder how rye-grass pollen could be an allergen, when it is too large to fit into the smaller airways in the lungs. A few years ago, the mechanism was worked out by a team of botanists and doctors from Melbourne.

It seems that when rye-grass pollen gets wet, the grain swells and ruptures, releasing about seven hundred starch granules. These granules are both highly allergenic and small enough to get into the airways.

# Other aeroallergens and irritants

Pollen is not the only aeroallergen. Many plants give off tiny bits of debris. Just as trees lose their bark, so many plants lose bits and pieces, some of which will be light enough to float on the breeze.

As well, there are many different substances floating through the air which can irritate the airways and trigger off asthma. And, while the links between pollution and asthma are unclear, all the particles in the air are likely to have some effect, even if it is only to irritate the airways.

**Industrial chemicals** such as phenylglycine and chloroplatinates can provoke asthma.

**Volcanic eruptions** scatter huge amounts of ash and microscopic particles into the air, many of which can provoke asthma.

**Waves** crashing on the rocks throw up tiny particles containing salty debris, which can provoke asthma.

**Cars** pour out hydrocarbons and lead.

**Power stations** emit coal dust.

**Factories** pump smoke into the skies.

## GO FOR THE SHOW

As a general rule, insect-pollinated plants are those that will cause less trouble for people with asthma and/or hayfever than wind-pollinated plants. And, as a general rule, insect-pollinated plants have large, showy flowers to attract the insects and birds on which they rely.

So if you want a simple rule to follow, and you want to plant a low allergy garden, then buy plants with large, flashy flowers, and ignore the demure ones. Go for the show. Not only do these flowers attract birds, but they attract gardeners!

# CHAPTER 5
# ASSESSING ALLERGIES

Many doctors involved with allergies recommend that if you have allergic or atopic symptoms – if you have asthma, hayfever, sinusitis or eczema – you should be assessed properly by a doctor with knowledge of allergies.

This requires more than just tests, although the tests are an important part of any assessment. The following steps are required.

## History

You should ask yourself what symptoms you have and when you have them.

- Are your symptoms worse at one time of the year than another – usually but not always spring?

- Do you get a runny nose at certain times of the year? Itchy eyes? Itchy mouth or ears? Asthma?

- Are your symptoms worse on windy days?

- Are your symptoms worse when you are inside the house? Or outside? Or somewhere else altogether?

- Do your symptoms change when you go on holidays?

- Are they worse when you lie on your sister's lounge, and find out that's where the cat sleeps?

If the answers to these types of questions are yes, then pollens may be causing some of your problems. You should see a doctor, who will run through the same types of questions, and then some more.

It would help if you could keep a chart or diary of your symptoms for a few months, while you are considering the issue. Look at the Daily Symptom Chart on pages 26 to 27, and fill it in for a while. You can chart on it symptoms such as:

- runny, itchy nose;
- sneezing;
- watery eyes;
- sore throat;
- asthma;
- stomach upset;
- eczema or hives.

## Skin prick tests

Skin prick tests are fairly simple tests to take. You bare your forearm to a doctor, who places drops of fluid on your arm. These drops each contain a different allergen extract.

The doctor then pricks the skin through each allergen extract, and you wait. After 15 minutes, the doctor measures the size of the reaction to the different allergen extracts.

A large red itchy lump suggests an allergy to that extract, while a small or non-existent reaction suggests you are not allergic to that extract.

## Blood tests

The blood test is also known as a RAST test, or Radio-Allergo-Sorbent Test. It measures the amount of specific antibodies in your blood. As well as highlighting specific allergies, it can give guidance as to how allergic you are, although it is not as reliable as properly interpreted skin tests.

# Symptom diary chart

| DAY | MONTH | | | | |
|---|---|---|---|---|---|
| 1 | | | | | |
| 2 | | | | | |
| 3 | | | | | |
| 4 | | | | | |
| 5 | | | | | |
| 6 | | | | | |
| 7 | | | | | |
| 8 | | | | | |
| 9 | | | | | |
| 10 | | | | | |
| 11 | | | | | |
| 12 | | | | | |
| 13 | | | | | |
| 14 | | | | | |
| 15 | | | | | |
| 16 | | | | | |
| 17 | | | | | |
| 18 | | | | | |
| 19 | | | | | |
| 20 | | | | | |
| 21 | | | | | |
| 22 | | | | | |
| 23 | | | | | |
| 24 | | | | | |
| 25 | | | | | |
| 26 | | | | | |
| 27 | | | | | |
| 28 | | | | | |
| 29 | | | | | |
| 30 | | | | | |
| 31 | | | | | |

# Symptom diary chart

### MONTH

| | | | | | |
|---|---|---|---|---|---|
| | | | | | |
| | | | | | |
| | | | | | |
| | | | | | |
| | | | | | |
| | | | | | |
| | | | | | |
| | | | | | |
| | | | | | |
| | | | | | |
| | | | | | |
| | | | | | |
| | | | | | |
| | | | | | |
| | | | | | |
| | | | | | |
| | | | | | |
| | | | | | |
| | | | | | |
| | | | | | |
| | | | | | |
| | | | | | |
| | | | | | |
| | | | | | |
| | | | | | |
| | | | | | |
| | | | | | |
| | | | | | |
| | | | | | |
| | | | | | |
| | | | | | |

**Use this chart to keep track of the symptoms you are suffering:**

For example:
• Runny, itchy
  nose
• Sneezing
• Watery eyes
• Sore throat
• Asthma
• Stomach upset
• Eczema or
  hives
• Coughing
• Wheezing

Note the month at the top of the column and the type of symptom in the box for the day.

# Tying it all together

It is important, once you have had all these tests, to tie in the results of the tests with your life. It is no use having a test say you are allergic to cats, when you know that you can pick up cats and cuddle them without any change in your condition.

Allergy tests are not always 100 per cent relevant. They give a good guidance to a good doctor, who will interpret them based on further questions and answers.

If it turns out that you are allergic to the house dust mite, as are many people, then you can find ways to reduce the dust in your house. I won't go into this in detail, as your local Asthma Foundation can provide all the information you need on house dust mites, but the aim is to get rid of articles on which dust can collect, such as soft furnishings, carpets, fluffy toys and so on. You also need to ventilate the house well, and stop it from getting too warm and humid.

If it turns out that you are allergic to grass pollens, as are many people, and it seems to tie in with what happens – your symptoms get worse when you mow the lawn – then you can deal with that.

If it turns out that you are allergic to particular plants, then you can deal with that by avoiding those plants and by putting in plants that are low allergen.

In all, if you are allergic to something that is making you feel worse, there is usually something you can do about it. The rest of this book will help you deal with allergies to plants and pollens.

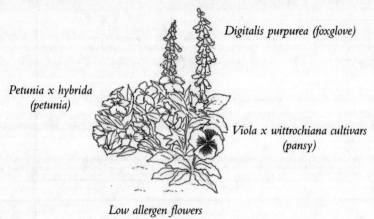

*Digitalis purpurea (foxglove)*

*Petunia x hybrida (petunia)*

*Viola x wittrochiana cultivars (pansy)*

*Low allergen flowers*

## PUTTING IT IN CONTEXT

About 40 per cent of Australians and New Zealanders will have positive results on the skin prick test, most commonly to grasses and dust mites.

If you are negative on the skin prick, then your asthma, hayfever or other problems are not caused by an allergy. You need to look to other remedies for your illness.

If you are positive, it still does not mean allergies have to be causing the problem. You need to examine your illness and see whether it could be based on allergies. You need common sense as well as test results.

# CHAPTER 6
# THE POLLEN SEASON

Australia and New Zealand have marked pollen seasons. The Pollen Charts for all the States of Australia and for New Zealand in this chapter will spell out the pollen seasons in great detail, but it is possible to generalise.

The pollen season usually begins towards the end of August, when trees start to give off their pollens. Some weed pollens follow soon after.

Tree pollen production hits its peak around the end of September and start of October, then the grass pollens take over. These reach a peak in November and December, although they usually drop off markedly in January. The level of grass pollen stays low for the rest of the year, apart from a small peak in February and sometimes in April or May.

Privet (*Ligustrum* spp.) sprays its pollen around in January and February, with another smaller pollen peak in September and October. Plantain (*Plantago* spp.), a common weed, spreads its pollen from September through to April.

*Ligustrum lucidum (privet)*

# JANUARY

| PLANT NAME | QLD | NSW | ACT | VIC | TAS | SA | WA | NT |
|---|---|---|---|---|---|---|---|---|
| Bermuda couch grass<br>*Cynodon dactylon* | | ● | ● | ● | | ● | ● | |
| Rye grass<br>*Lolium perenne* | | ● | ● | | | ● *little* | | |
| Prairie grass<br>*Bromus uniloides* | ● | | | | | | | |
| Cocksfoot/Orchard<br>*Dactylis glomerata* | | ● | ● | | | | | |
| Johnson grass<br>*Sorghum halipense* | ● | ● | ● | | | | | |
| Rhodes grass<br>*Chloris gayana* | ● | ● | ● | | | | | |
| Kikuyu grass<br>*Pennisetum clandestinum* | ● | ● | ● | | | | | |
| Kangaroo grass<br>*Thermeda australis* | ● | ● | ● | | | | | |
| Buffel grass<br>*Centrus cilaris* | ● | | | | | | | |
| Red Natal grass<br>*Rhynchelytrum repens* | ● | ● | ● | | | | | |
| Paspalum grass<br>*Paspalum dilatatum* | | ● | ● | ● | | | | |
| Wattle<br>*Acacia* spp. | | ● | ● | | | | | |
| She oak<br>*Casuarina* spp. | | ● | ● | | | | | |
| Eucalypts<br>*Myrtaceae* spp. | | ● | ● | | | ● | ● | |
| Elm<br>*Ulmus* spp. | | ● | ● | | | | | |
| Oak<br>*Quercus* spp. | | ● | ● | | | | | |
| Privet (large leaf)<br>*Ligustrum lucidum* | | ● | ● | ● | | | | |
| Melaleuca<br>*Myrtaceae* spp. | | ● | ● | | | | | |
| Plantain<br>*Plantago lanceolatum* | ● | ● | ● | ● | | ● | | |
| Dock/Sorrel<br>*Rumex crispus/acetosella* | ● | | | ● *early* | | | | |
| Fat hen<br>*Chenopodium album* | | ● | ● | ● | | ● | | |
| Pellitory<br>*Parietaria judaica* | | ●●<br>*Sydney* | | | | | | |

# FEBRUARY

| Plant Name | QLD | NSW | ACT | VIC | TAS | SA | WA | NT |
|---|---|---|---|---|---|---|---|---|
| Bermuda couch gras<br>*Cynodon dactylon* | | ● | ● | ● | | ● | ● | |
| Rye grass<br>*Lolium perenne* | | ● | ● | ● | | ● *little* | | |
| Canary grass<br>*Phalaris* spp. | | | | ● | | | | |
| Prairie grass<br>*Bromus uniloides* | ● | | | | | | | |
| Cocksfoot/Orchard grass<br>*Dactylis glomerata* | | ● | ● | | | | | |
| Johnson grass<br>*Sorghum halipense* | ● | | | | | | | |
| Rhodes grass<br>*Chloris gayana* | ● | ● | ● | | | | | |
| Kangaroo grass<br>*Thermeda australis* | | ● | ● | ● | | | | |
| Buffel grass<br>*Centrus cilaris* | ● | | | | | | | |
| Guinea grass<br>*Panicum maximum* | ● | | | | | | | |
| Red Natal grass<br>*Rhynchelytrum repens* | ● | ● | ● | | | | | |
| Paspalum grass<br>*Paspalum dilatatum* | | ● | ● | ● | | ● | | |
| Wattle<br>*Acacia* spp. | | ● | ● | | | | | |
| She oak<br>*Casuarina* spp. | | ● | ● | | | | | |
| Eucalypts<br>*Myrtaceae* spp. | | ● | ● | | | ● | ● | |
| Melaleuca<br>*Myrtaceae* spp. | | ● | ● | | | | | |
| Plantain<br>*Plantago lanceolatum* | ● | ● | ● | ● | | ● | | |
| Dock/Sorrel<br>*Rumex crispus/acetosella* | ● | ● | ● | | | | | |
| Fat hen<br>*Chenopodium album* | ● | ● | ● | ● | | ● | | |
| Pellitory<br>*Parietaria judaica* | | ●● *Sydney* | | | | | | |

# MARCH

| Plant Name | Qld | NSW | ACT | Vic | Tas | SA | WA | NT |
|---|---|---|---|---|---|---|---|---|
| Bermuda couch grass<br>*Cynodon dactylon* | | ● | ● | | | ● | ● | |
| Rye grass<br>*Lolium perenne* | | | | | | little | | |
| Prairie grass<br>*Bromus uniloides* | ● | | | | | | | |
| Rhodes grass<br>*Chloris gayana* | ● | ● | ● | | | | | |
| Kangaroo grass<br>*Thermeda australis* | | ● | ● | | | | | |
| Red Natal grass<br>*Rhynchelytrum repens* | ● | ● | ● | | | | | |
| Paspalum grass<br>*Paspalum dilatatum* | | ● | ● | ● | ● | | | |
| Wattle<br>*Acacia* spp. | | ● | ● | | | | | |
| She oak<br>*Casuarina* spp. | | ● | ● | ● | | | | |
| Eucalypts<br>*Myrtaceae* spp. | | ● | ● | | | ● | | |
| Melaleuca<br>*Myrtaceae* spp. | | ● | ● | | | | | |
| Cedrus deodora | | ● | ● | | | | | |
| Plantain<br>*Plantago lanceolatum* | ● | | | ● | | ● | | |
| Dock/Sorrel<br>*Rumex crispus/acetosella* | ● | ● | ● | | | | | |
| Fat hen<br>*Chenopodium album* | ● | ● | ● | ● | | ● | | |
| Perennial Ragweed<br>*Ambrosia psilostachya* | | ● | ● | | | | | |
| Lambs quarters<br>*Amaranth* spp. | | | | | | ● | | |
| Pellitory<br>*Parietaria judaica* | | ●●<br>*Sydney* | | | | | | |

# APRIL

| Plant Name | QLD | NSW | ACT | VIC | TAS | SA | WA | NT |
|---|---|---|---|---|---|---|---|---|
| Bermuda couch Grass *Cynodon dactylon* | | ● | ● | ● | | | | |
| Annual blue grass *Poa annua* | | | | ● | | | | |
| Rhodes grass *Chloris gayana* | ● | ● | ● | | | | | |
| Kangaroo grass *Thermeda australis* | | ● | ● | | | | | |
| Guinea grass *Panicum maximum* | ● | | | | | | | |
| Red Natal grass *Rhynchelytrum repens* | ● | ● | ● | | | | | |
| Paspalum grass *Paspalum dilatatum* | | ● | ● | | | | | |
| Wattle *Acacia* spp. | | ● | ● | ● | | | | |
| She oak *Casuarina* spp. | | ● | ● | ● | | | | |
| Eucalypts *Myrtaceae* spp. | | ● | ● | | | ● | | |
| Melaleuca *Myrtaceae* spp. | | ● | ● | | | | | |
| Cedrus deodora | | ● | ● | | | | | |
| Dock/Sorrel *Rumex crispus/acetosella* | | ● | ● | | | | | |
| Fat hen *Chenopodium album* | ● | ● | ● | ● | | ● | | |
| Perennial Ragweed *Ambrosia psilostachya* | ● | ● | ● | | | | | |
| Lambs quarters *Amaranth* spp. | | | | | | ● | | |
| Pellitory *Parietaria judaica* | | ● Sydney | | | | | | |

## MAY

| Plant Name | Qld | NSW | ACT | Vic | Tas | SA | WA | NT |
|---|---|---|---|---|---|---|---|---|
| Bermuda couch grass *Cynodon dactylon* | | ● | ● | | | | | |
| Annual blue grass *Poa annua* | | | | ● | | | | |
| Wild oat *Avena fatua* | | ● | ● | | | | | |
| Rhodes grass *Chloris gayana* | ● | ● | ● | | | | | |
| Kangaroo grass *Thermeda australis* | | ● | ● | | | | | |
| Red Natal grass *Rhynchelytrum repens* | ● | ● | ● | | | | | |
| Wattle *Acacia* spp. | | ● | ● | | | | | |
| Eucalypts *Myrtaceae* spp. | | ● | ● | | | ● | | |
| Monterey pine *Pinus radiata* | | ● | ● | | | | | |
| Cedrus deodora | | ● | ● | | | | | |

# JUNE

| PLANT NAME | QLD | NSW | ACT | VIC | TAS | SA | WA | NT |
|---|---|---|---|---|---|---|---|---|
| Annual blue grass<br>*Poa annua* | | | | ● | | | ● | |
| Wild oat<br>*Avena fatua* | | ● | ● | | | | | |
| Red Natal grass<br>*Rhynchelytrum repens* | ● | ● | ● | | | | | |
| Eucalypts<br>*Myrtaceae* spp. | | | | | | ● | | |
| Murray/Cypress pine<br>*Callitris* spp. | | | | ● | | | | |
| Monterey pine<br>*Pinus radiata* | | | | ● | | | | |
| Golden Cypress<br>*Cypressus* spp. | | ● | ● | ● | | | | |
| Ash<br>*Fraxinus* spp. | | | | | | ● | | |
| Plantain<br>*Plantago lanceolatum* | | ●little | ●little | | | | | |
| Pellitory<br>*Parietaria judaica* | | ●little | ●little | | | | | |

# JULY

| Plant Name | QLD | NSW | ACT | VIC | TAS | SA | WA | NT |
|---|---|---|---|---|---|---|---|---|
| Annual blue grass<br>*Poa annua* | | ● | ● | ● | | ● | | |
| Wild oat<br>*Avena fatua* | | ● | ● | | | ● | | |
| Wattle<br>*Acacia* spp. | | | | | | ● | | |
| She oak<br>*Casuarina* spp. | | ● | ● | | | | ● | |
| Eucalypts<br>*Myrtaceae* spp. | | | | | | ● | | |
| Murray/Cypress pine<br>*Callitris* spp. | | | | ● | | | | |
| Monterey pine<br>*Pinus radiata* | | | | ● | | | ● | |
| Golden Cypress<br>*Cypressus* spp. | | ● | ● | ● | | | | |
| Ash<br>*Fraxinus* spp. | | ● | ● | | | ● | | |
| Elm<br>*Ulmus* spp. | | ● | ● | | | | | |
| Plantain<br>*Plantago lanceolatum* | | ● little | ● little | | | | | |
| Pellitory<br>*Parietaria judaica* | | ● little<br>Sydney | | | | | | |

## AUGUST

| Plant Name | QLD | NSW | ACT | VIC | TAS | SA | WA | NT |
|---|---|---|---|---|---|---|---|---|
| Bermuda couch grass *Cynodon dactylon* | | ● | ● | | | | | |
| Annual blue grass *Poa annua* | | ● | ● | ● | | ● | | |
| Canary grass *Phalaris* spp. | ● | | | | | | | |
| Prairie grass *Bromus uniloides* | ● | ● | ● | | | | | |
| Wild oat *Avena fatua* | | ● | ● | | | ● | | |
| Barley grass *Hordeum leporinum* | | ● | ● | | | | | |
| Sweet vernal grass *Anthoxanthum odoratum* | | ● | ● | | | | | |
| Buffel grass *Centrus cilaris* | ● | | | | | | | |
| Guinea grass *Panicum maximum* | ● | | | | | | | |
| Red Natal grass *Rhynchelytrum repens* | ● | | | | | | | |
| Wattle *Acacia* spp. | ● | ● | ● | | | ● | | |
| She oak *Casuarina* spp. | | ● | ● | | | | ● | |
| Eucalypts *Myrtaceae* spp. | | ● | ● | | | ● | | |
| Murray/Cypress pine *Callitris* spp. | | ● | ● | ● | | ● | ● | |
| Monterey pine *Pinus radiata* | ● | ● | ● | ● | | ● | ● | |
| Golden cypress *Cupressus* spp. | ● | ● | ● | ● | | ● | ● | |
| Ash *Fraxinus* spp. | | ● | ● | ● | | ● | | |
| Plane *Plantanus* spp. | ● | ● | ● | | | | | |
| Elm *Ulmus* spp. | ● | ● | ● | ● | | ● | | |
| Oak *Quercus* spp. | | ● | ● | | | | | |
| Poplar *Populus deltoides* | | ● | ● | | | | | |
| Plantain *Plantago lanceolatum* | ● | ● | ● | | | | | |
| Dock/Sorrel *Rumex crispus/acetosella* | ● | ● | ● | | | | | |
| Pellitory *Parietaria judaica* | | ● Sydney | | | | | | |

# SEPTEMBER

| PLANT NAME | QLD | NSW | ACT | VIC | TAS | SA | WA | NT |
|---|---|---|---|---|---|---|---|---|
| Bermuda couch grass *Cynodon dactylon* | ● | ● | ● | | | | | |
| Annual blue grass *Poa annua* | | ● | ● | ● | | ● | ● | |
| Rye grass *Lolium perenne* | | ● | ● | | | | ● | |
| Prairie grass *Bromus uniloides* | ● | ● | ● | | | | | |
| Cocksfoot/Orchard grass *Dactylis glomerata* | | ● | ● | ● | | | | |
| Wild oat *Avena fatua* | | ● | ● | | | ● | | |
| Barley grass *Hordeum leporinum* | | ● | ● | | | | | |
| Sweet vernal grass *Anthoxanthum odoratum* | | ● | ● | | | | | |
| Rhodes grass *Chloris gayana* | ● | | | | | | | |
| Kikuyu grass *Pennisetum clandestinum* | ● | | | | | | | |
| Buffel grass *Centrus cilaris* | ● | | | | | | | |
| Veldt grass *Ehrharta calycina* | | | | ● | | ● | ● | |
| Timothy grass *Phleum pratense* | | | | | ● | | | |
| Wattle *Acacia* spp. | ● | ● | ● | | ● | ● | | |
| She oak *Casuarina* spp. | | ● | ● | | | ● | | |
| Eucalypts *Myrtaceae* spp. | | ● | ● | | | | ● | |
| Murray/Cypress pine *Callitris* spp. | | ● | ● | | | ● | ● | |
| Monterey pine *Pinus radiata* | ● | ● | ● | | | ● | ● | |
| Golden cypress *Cypressus* spp. | ● | ● | ● | ● | | ● | ● | |
| Silver birch *Betula* spp. | | ● | ● | ● | ● | | | |
| Alder *Alnus* spp. | | ● | ● | | | | | |
| Maple *Acer* spp. | | ● | ● | | | | | |

# SEPTEMBER

| Plant Name | Qld | NSW | ACT | Vic | Tas | SA | WA | NT |
|---|---|---|---|---|---|---|---|---|
| Ash<br>*Fraxinus* spp. | | | | | | ● | | |
| Plane<br>*Plantanus* spp. | ● | ● | ● | ● | | ● | | |
| Elm<br>*Ulmus* spp. | ● | ● | ● | ● | ● | early | | |
| Oak<br>*Quercus* spp. | | ● | ● | ●end | ● | | | |
| Olive<br>*Oleaece* spp. | | | | ● | | | | |
| Willow<br>*Salix* spp. | | ● | ● | | | | | |
| Poplar<br>*Populus deltoides* | | ● | ● | | | | | |
| Plantain<br>*Plantago lanceolatum* | ● | ● | ● | | | ● | | |
| Salvation Jane Patersons curse<br>*Echium plantagineum* | | ●● | ●● | ●● | | ●● | | |
| Dock/Sorrel<br>*Rumex crispus/acetosella* | | ● | ● | ● | | | | |
| Pellitory<br>*Parietaria judaica* | | ●●<br>Sydney | | | | | | |

# OCTOBER

| Plant Name | QLD | NSW | ACT | VIC | TAS | SA | WA | NT |
|---|---|---|---|---|---|---|---|---|
| Bermuda couch grass *Cynodon dactylon* | | ● | ● | | ● | ● | | |
| Annual blue grass *Poa annua* | | ● | ● | ● | | ● | | |
| Rye grass *Lolium perenne* | | ● | ● | ● | ● | | ● | |
| Kentucky blue/June grass *Poa pratense* | | ● | ● | ● | ● | ● | | |
| Canary grass *Phalaris* spp. | | ● | ● | | | | ● | |
| Prairie grass *Bromus uniloides* | ● | ● | ● | | | | | |
| Cocksfoot/Orchard grass *Dactylis glomerata* | | ● | ● | ● | | | ● | |
| Wild oat *Avena fatua* | | ● | ● | ● | ● | ● | ● | |
| Barley grass *Hordeum leporinum* | | ● | ● | ● | | ● | ● | |
| Sweet vernal grass *Anthoxanthum odoratum* | | ● | ● | ● | ● | | | |
| Johnson grass *Sorghum halipense* | ● | | | | | | | |
| Rhodes grass *Chloris gayana* | ● | | | | | | | |
| Kikuyu grass *Pennisetum clandestinum* | ● | | | | | | | |
| Kangaroo grass *Thermeda australis* | | | | ● | | | | |
| Buffel grass *Centrus cilaris* | ● | | | | | | | |
| Veldt grass *Ehrharta calycina* | | | | | | ● | | |
| Timothy grass *Phleum pratense* | | | | ● | ● | | | |
| Wattle *Acacia* spp. | ● | ● | ● | ● | ● | ● | | |
| She oak *Casuarina* spp. | | ● | ● | | | | | |
| Eucalypts *Myrtaceae* spp. | | ● | ● | ● | ● | | ● | |
| Murray/Cypress pine *Callitris* spp. | ● | ● | ● | ● | | ● | | |
| Golden cypress *Cypressus* spp. | ● | ● | ● | ● | | ● | ● | |

# OCTOBER

| Plant Name | QLD | NSW | ACT | VIC | TAS | SA | WA | NT |
|---|---|---|---|---|---|---|---|---|
| Silver birch<br>*Betula* spp. | | ● | ● | | ● | ● | | |
| Maple<br>*Acer* spp. | | ● | ● | | ● | | | |
| Plane<br>*Plantanus* spp. | ● | | | ● | | | | |
| Olive<br>*Oleaece* spp. | ● | ● | ● | ● | | | | |
| Privet (small leaf)<br>*Ligustrum sinense* | | ● | ● | | | | | |
| Poplar<br>*Populus deltoides* | | ● | ● | ● | | | | |
| Plantain<br>*Plantago lanceolatum* | ● | ●●● | ●●● | ●*late* | ● | ● | ● | |
| Salvation Jane Patersons curse<br>*Echium plantagineum* | | ● | ● | ● | | ● | ● | |
| Dock/Sorrel<br>*Rumex crispus/acetosella* | | ● | ● | ● | | | | |
| Fat hen<br>*Chenopodium album* | | | | | | ● | | |
| Pellitory<br>*Parietaria judaica* | | ●●●<br>*Sydney* | | | | | | |

# NOVEMBER

| Plant Name | QLD | NSW | ACT | VIC | TAS | SA | WA | NT |
|---|---|---|---|---|---|---|---|---|
| Bermuda couch grass *Cynodon dactylon* | • | • | • | | • | • | | |
| Annual blue grass *Poa annua* | | • | • | | | • | | |
| Rye grass *Lolium perenne* | | •• | •• | •• | • | •• | • | |
| Kentucky blue/June grass *Poa pratense* | | • | • | • | | • | | |
| Canary grass *Phalaris* spp. | | • | • | | | | • | |
| Prairie grass *Bromus uniloides* | • | • | • | • | | | | |
| Cocksfoot/Orchard grass *Dactylis glomerata* | | • | • | • | • | | | |
| Wild oat *Avena fatua* | | • | • | • | • | • | • | |
| Barley grass *Hordeum leporinum* | | | | | | • | • | |
| Sweet vernal grass *Anthoxanthum odoratum* | | • | • | • | • | | | |
| Johnson grass *Sorghum halipense* | • | | | | | | | |
| Rhodes grass *Chloris gayana* | • | | | | | | | |
| Kikuyu grass *Pennisetum clandestinum* | • | | | | | | | |
| Buffel grass *Centrus cilaris* | • | | | | | | | |
| Veldt grass *Ehrharta calycina* | | | | | | • | | |
| Red Natal grass *Rhynchelytrum repens* | • | | | | | | | |
| Paspalum grass *Paspalum dilatatum* | | • | • | | | | | |
| Timothy grass *Phleum pratense* | | | | | • | | | |
| Wattle *Acacia* spp. | | • | • | • | | • | • | |
| She oak *Casuarina* spp. | | • | • | | | | • | |
| Eucalypts *Myrtaceae* spp. | | • | • | • | | • | • | |
| Murray/Cypress pine *Callitris* spp. | | | | | | | | |

# NOVEMBER

| PLANT NAME | QLD | NSW | ACT | VIC | TAS | SA | WA | NT |
|---|---|---|---|---|---|---|---|---|
| Golden cypress<br>*Cypressus* spp. | | | | ● | | ● | ● | |
| Silver birch<br>*Betula* spp. | | | | | | ● | | |
| Olive<br>*Oleaece* spp. | | ● | ● | ● | | | | |
| Privet (small leaf)<br>*Ligustrum sinense* | | | | ● | | | | |
| Poplar<br>*Populus deltoides* | | ● | ● | | | | | |
| Plantain<br>*Plantago lanceolatum* | ● | ● | ● | ● | | ● | | |
| Salvation Jane Patersons curse<br>*Echium plantagineum* | | ●● | ●● | | | ●● | ● North | |
| Dock/Sorrel<br>*Rumex crispus/acetosella* | | ● | ● | | | | | |
| Fat hen<br>*Chenopodium album* | | | | | | ● | | |
| Capeweed<br>*Arctotheca calendula* | | ● | ● | | | | | |
| Pellitory<br>*Parietaria judaica* | | ●●●<br>Sydney | | | | | | |

# DECEMBER

| Plant Name | Qld | NSW | ACT | Vic | Tas | SA | WA | NT |
|---|---|---|---|---|---|---|---|---|
| Bermuda couch grass<br>*Cynodon dactylon* | ● | ● | ● | | ● | ● | ● | |
| Annual blue grass<br>*Poa annua* | | | | | | ● | | |
| Rye grass<br>*Lolium perenne* | | ● | ● | ● | ● | ● | | |
| Kentucky blue/June grass<br>*Poa pratense* | | ● | ● | | | ● | | |
| Canary grass<br>*Phalaris* spp. | | ● | ● | ● | | | | |
| Prairie grass<br>*Bromus uniloides* | ● | ● | ● | | | | | |
| Cocksfoot/Orchard grass<br>*Dactylis glomerata* | | ● | ● | ● | ● | | | |
| Wild oa<br>*Avena fatua* | | ● | ● | ● | ● | ● | | |
| Barley grass<br>*Hordeum leporinum* | | | | | | ● | | |
| Sweet vernal grass<br>*Anthoxanthum odoratum* | | | | | ● | | | |
| Johnson grass<br>*Sorghum halipense* | ● | ● | ● | | | | | |
| Rhodes grass<br>*Chloris gayana* | ● | ● | ● | | | | | |
| Kikuyu grass<br>*Pennisetum clandestinum* | ● | | | | | | | |
| Kangaroo grass<br>*Thermeda australis* | ● | ● | ● | | | | | |
| Buffel grass<br>*Centrus cilaris* | ● | | | | | | | |
| Guinea grass<br>*Panicum maximum* | ● | | | | | | | |
| Red Natal grass<br>*Rhynchelytrum repens* | ● | ● | ● | | | | | |
| Paspalum grass<br>*Paspalum dilatatum* | | ● | ● | ● | | | | |
| Wattle<br>*Acacia* spp. | | ● | ● | | | | | |
| She oak<br>*Casuarina* spp. | | ● | ● | | | | | |
| Eucalypts<br>*Myrtaceae* spp. | | ● | ● | | | ● | ● | |
| Monterey pine<br>*Pinus radiata* | | ●early | ●early | | | ● | ● | |

# DECEMBER

| PLANT NAME | QLD | NSW | ACT | VIC | TAS | SA | WA | NT |
|---|---|---|---|---|---|---|---|---|
| Privet (large leaf) *Ligustrum lucidum* | | ● | ● | | | | | |
| Melaleuca *Myrtaceae* spp. | | ● | ● | | | | | |
| Plantain *Plantago lanceolatum* | ● | ● | ● | ● | | ● | | |
| Salvation Jane Patersons curse *Echium plantagineum* | | ● | ● | ● | | ● | | |
| Dock/Sorrel *Rumex crispus/acetosella* | ● | ● | ● | ● | | | | |
| Fat hen *Chenopodium album* | | | | | | ● | | |
| Perennial Ragweed *Ambrosia psilostachya* | | ● | ● | | | | | |
| Wild mustard *Daucus carota* | | ● | ● | | | | | |
| Pellitory *Parietaria judaica* | | ●●● Sydney | | | | | | |

# NEW ZEALAND POLLEN CALENDAR

| SPECIES | JAN | FEB | MAR | APR | MAY | JUN | JUL | AUG | SEP | OCT | NOV | DEC |
|---|---|---|---|---|---|---|---|---|---|---|---|---|
| Wattle *Acacia* | | | | | | ● | ● | ● | ● | ● | ● | |
| Macrocarpa ★ *Cupressus* | ● | ● | | | | ● | ● | ● | ● | ● | ● | ● |
| Pinus radiata ★ | | | | | | | ● | ● | ● | | | |
| Hazelnut *Corylus* | | | | | | | ● | ● | ● | | | |
| Gorse ★+ *Ulex* | | | ● | ● | ● | ● | ● | ● | ● | ● | ● | |
| Willow *Salix* | | | | | | | | ● | ● | ● | | |
| Alder *Alnus* | | | | | | | | ● | ● | | | |
| Poplar *Populus* | | | | | | | | ● | ● | ● | | |
| Meadow Foxtail *Alopecurus* | ● | | | | | | | | ● | ● | ● | ● |
| Other Pinus species ★ | | | | | | | | | ● | ● | ● | ● |
| Oak *Quercus* | | | | | | | | | ● | ● | ● | |
| Native Beech ★ *Nothofagus* | ● | | | | | | | | ● | ● | ● | ● |
| Coproma species ★ | | | | | | | | | ● | ● | ● | |
| Elm *Ulmus* | | | | | | | | | ● | ● | ● | |
| Maples, Sycamore *Acer* | | | | | | | | | ● | ● | ● | |
| Birch *Betula* | | | | | | | | | ● late | ● | ● | |
| Plane *Platanus* | | | | | | | | | | ● | ● | |
| Walnut *Juglans* | | | | | | | | | | ● | ● | |
| Mulberry *Morus* | | | | | | | | | | ● | ● | |
| Plantain *Plantago* | ● | ● | ● early | | | | | | | ● | ● | ● |
| Sweet Vernal *Anthoxanthum* | ● | | | | | | | | | ● | ● | ● |
| Cocksfoot *Dactylis* | ● | | | | | | | | | | ● | ● |
| Yorkshire Fog *Holcus* | ● | | | | | | | | | ● | ● | ● |

# NEW ZEALAND POLLEN CALENDAR

| SPECIES | JAN | FEB | MAR | APR | MAY | JUN | JUL | AUG | SEP | OCT | NOV | DEC |
|---|---|---|---|---|---|---|---|---|---|---|---|---|
| Ryegrass *Lolium* | ● | ● | | | | | | | | | ● | ● |
| Native Podocarps (e.g. Rimu) ★ | ● | | | | | | | | | | ● | ● |
| Eucalypts/Manuka ★ | ● | | | | | | | | | | ● | ● |
| Hedge Privet + *Ligustrum* | ● | | | | | | | | | | ● | ● |
| Native Milkwoods ★ | ● | | | | | | | | | | ● | ● |
| Nettles *Urtica* | ● | | | | | | | | | ● | ● | ● |
| Dock, Sorrel *Rumex* | ● | ● | ● | | | | | | | ● late | ● | ● |
| Artemisia | ● | | | | | | | | | | ● | ● |
| Tall Fescue *Festuca* | ● | | | | | | | | | ● | ● | ● |
| Prairie grass *Bromus* | ● | | | | | | | | | | ● | ● |
| Dogstail *Cynosurus* | ● | ● | | | | | | | | | | ● |
| Browntop *Agrostis* | ● | ● | | | | | | | | | | ● |
| Pohutukawa/Rata *Metrosideros* | ● | ● | ● | | | | | | | | | ● |
| Chenopod Weeds (e.g. fathen) | ● | ● | ● | | | | | | | | ● late | ● |
| Crested Dogstail *Cynosurus* | ● | ● | | | | | | | | | | ● |
| Timothy *Phleum* | ● | ● | | | | | | | | | | ● |
| Fungul spores | ● | ● | ● | ● | ● | ● | ● | ● | ● | | | ● |
| Fern spores ★ | | | | | | | | | | ● | ● | ● |
| Tree privet + | | ● | ● | | | | | | | | | |
| Bullrush *Typha* | ● | ● | | | | | | | | | | |

★ Suspected to be allergenic.

+ The scent may be allergy/asthma provoking.

*Reproduced courtesy Dr David Fountain, Astra New Zealand Limited and the Auckland Asthma Society Inc.*

# Part II
# PLANTS TO CHOOSE FOR YOUR LOW ALLERGY GARDEN

Flowers • Shrubs • Trees • Grasses •

Ground Cover • Climbers • Herbs

# CHAPTER 7
# FLOWERS

Flowers are the bright and showy parts of the garden. Among all that green (and, if you're not that hot in the garden, brown), it is lovely to have flowers to add life and colour.

You can do all sorts of things with gardens to create a good show. You can plant perennials which require some care, or annuals which need a bit more love and regular replanting.

You can go for all low flowers to highlight the sweep of a beautifully crafted sandstone or paved pathway, or you can mix heights to provide variety and an element of surprise.

You can go for the delicate, wispy look with fine-stemmed small-petalled flowers, or you can choose a large, brash look.

You can go for a monochrome colour scheme, and plant only blue flowers, or only yellow, or white, or green with pink spots, if you can manage it. It seems to me to be a bit boring, like having a garden full of azaleas, but some people like it.

Whatever you choose, flowers can be a large part of a low allergy garden. After all, large showy flowers have evolved to attract birds and insects, and they are generally non-allergenic. So a low allergy garden is, almost by definition, a flower-filled garden.

*Begonia corallina (begonia)*

# Flowers to choose

## *Ageratum* (floss flower)

Small long-lasting annuals with deep lavender or white flowers. Sow or plant in spring for flowers through summer. May grow in winter in areas like northern Australia. Grows well in a window box.

## *Alyssum*

There are two main varieties of Alyssum found in gardens – sweet Alice and *Aurinia saxatilis*.

Sweet Alice grows almost anywhere – as a garden border, in rockeries or to add colour to sandstone flagging or between the stone of rough paths. You can get it in white, lavender and pink. Sweet Alice is quite hardy, and will grow in anything from full sun to near full shade. It spreads well, forming an attractive ground cover. Although it is classed as an annual, sweet Alice self-seeds readily and will hang around for years, although it can get a bit weedy as the years go by.

*Aurinia saxatilis* is a perennial that needs a cool climate. It has long grey leaves and tiny yellow flowers in spring. It usually grows to 20 centimetres high, and suffers badly from damp.

## *Anemone* spp.

The many varieties of Anemone are low spreading perennials, although many gardeners treat them as annuals by ripping them up after flowering. They have long stemmed, large, quite beautiful flowers of white, purple, blue or pink. They prefer partly shaded positions, and most of them need plenty of water. Some varieties are frost resistant, while others are not. They propagate well by division, and spread easily.

The sap of *Pulsatilla vulgaris* (eastern flower or pasque flower) is strongly alkaline and will blister the skin.

## *Antirrhinum majus* (snapdragon)

The snapdragon is a tallish striking annual with flowers of red, orange, yellow or white growing along the upper part of the stem. It likes full sun. The snapdragon can be quite fiddly for most gardeners to grow, being susceptible to fungal diseases.

## *Aquilegia* (columbine)

Aquilegia are squat perennials with unusual, five-leafed flowers in blue, white, purple, yellow, magenta and almost any other colour. In most parts of Australia and New Zealand, they grow best in light shade or dappled sunlight. They like to be protected from the wind and prefer a cool climate.

## *Begonia* spp.

Begonias are native of South America, mainly Brazil and Chile, but they have taken to Australia and New Zealand as if a native plant. Most prefer the conditions you imagine would exist in Brazil – warm, partly shaded under a canopy and with plenty of water, although they suffer from fungal diseases in humid conditions.

You can get Begonias in all shapes and sizes. The eyelash Begonia (*Begonia bowerae*) is a low plant with tiny pink flowers, while the coral Begonia (*Begonia corallina*) reaches 2.5 metres high. There are annual Begonias and there is a tree Begonia, *B. corallina*, which flowers almost throughout the year.

There are tuberous varieties, which grow in cool climates. They give spectacular flowers, then die down to a tuber.

Flowers vary in colour, but generally appear in summer. Many varieties have leaves that are coloured, whether that be red, lime, yellow or black, for a fair part of the year.

Refer also to Chapter 16 for details of this species.

## Bulbs

On the whole, bulbs are good for people with allergies, although the actual bulb can sometimes cause contact dermatitis. You can get bulbs of all colours, shapes and sizes, to flower in all seasons. They make a wonderful addition to any garden. While many bulbs prefer cooler climes, there is a large range of bulbs from the Cape region of South Africa which love hot, dry, sunny positions.

## Centaurea cyanus (cornflower)

Small annuals which provide beautiful deep blue flowers, perfect for posies. Need plenty of sun and well drained soil. Flower in summer. Prefer a cool climate.

## Clarkia spp.

Clarkia are small annuals with deep green leaves and pink, purple or white flowers in summer. Seeds are sown in autumn. They prefer the sun, but are sensitive to drought. The well-known annual known as farewell to spring, with its fragrant white flowers, is a Clarkia.

## Coleus, see Solenostemon scutellarioides cultivars

## Cornflower, see Centaurea cyanus

## Delphinium (Larkspur)

Delphiniums are large showy annuals which love a cool dry climate, mostly being natives of places like Tibet, Siberia, Nepal and other parts of central Asia where a frost is not unknown. They dislike humidity. Many small blue flowers appear along the tips of the stems in summer. They grow well in clusters and should self-seed.

## Dianthus barbatus (sweet William)

Sweet William is a small perennial or annual with deep green leaves and clusters of purple, red or pink flowers at the tips of erect stems. Closely bunched, they make impressive and long-lasting cut flowers. Sweet William prefers plenty of sun and is quite hardy.

## Digitalis purpurea (foxglove)

Foxglove is a biennial or short-lived perennial with leaves 30 centimetres long and tall spires of pink bell-shaped flowers in the second year. It doesn't like drought and, in warm climates, prefers light shade or dappled sunlight. There are annual varieties.

The foxglove is the source of one of the oldest Western medicines still in regular use. Its leaves are the source of digoxin, a drug used to treat heart failure (or dropsy as it was known then) since the eighteenth century. But high doses of digoxin are toxic, even fatal, so the plant itself must be considered highly poisonous if eaten.

## Foxglove see, *Digitalis purpurea*

## *Impatiens* spp.

Impatiens are smallish, succulent evergreen plants with bright coloured flowers of various hues. The best known species is busy Lizzie (*I. wallerana*), which came originally from tropical eastern Africa and has spread through Australian and New Zealand gardens wherever there is a damp spot and a bit of shade. Impatiens wilt in the summer sun, but will be revived if you spit on them.

They are easy to propagate. One way is to not clean a path – busy Lizzie will probably spring up within weeks. You can hack them back and the cuttings grow where they are left to lie. In the right conditions they seem like the model for the triffids – always growing, always sucking up moisture, always seeking new territory to dominate.

They make a wonderful cover-up for a dark nasty corner of the garden, or for that path down the side of the house where the sun never really reaches.

The newer dwarf varieties are not quite as prolific, and don't become as weedy as the older varieties can be. New Guinea varieties can handle the sun more readily, and some have attractive variegated leaves.

## *Linaria vulgaris* (toadflax)

This plant looks like the snapdragon, except that it is perennial and the flowers are very small and yellow. It self-seeds, but can become quite weedy.

## *Lobelia* spp.

You can get all types of Lobelia, from 4 metre shrubs that come from Mount Kilimanjaro to the blue Lobelia (*Lobelia erinus*) that most of us know. This is the tiny creeping herb, no more than 15 centimetres high and 30 centimetres across, that so many people use as a border for their gardens. Their small sharp leaves and masses of flowers suit either a cottage garden or a more formal approach, and can even be grown in a window box.

Although there are other varieties, it is the deep blue flowers that make this such a popular plant. The colour is so vivid that in the moonlight it almost seems to be giving off its own light.

## Nasturtium, see *Tropaeolum* spp.

### *Nemesia strumosa*
A small, pretty annual with erect leaves and multi-coloured, bell-shaped flowers.

## Pansy, see *Viola* x *wittrockiana* cultivars

### *Petunia* x *hybrida* (Petunia)
Petunias are pretty annuals which provide a squall of summer colour in pinks, blues, purples, reds, yellows, white and two-tones. They love the heat, and flower better if not watered from above. Petunias also grow well in a window box.

If you cut Petunias back hard when they become leggy, you often get a second, third or fourth flowering.

### *Phlox* spp.
Phlox are cool climate perennials or annuals from the mountains of North America. They have pretty tubular flowers which open into five petals. Colours range from white to pinks and soft purples. *Phlox speciosa* grows to 2 metres, while *Phlox stolonifera* is a creeper and *Phlox hoodii* barely gets off the ground. Most varieties, however, are small shrubs from 30 centimetres to 50 centimetres. Divide them in autumn to encourage growth. The annuals prefer cool, moist summers without humidity.

**Snapdragon, see *Antirrhinum majus***

## *Solenostemon scutellarioides* cultivars (coleus)

Coleus are rather sensitive souls, not being fond of wind, drought, frost or full sun. They are fleshy, succulent plants which demand rich soils and plenty of water. The Israeli rainbow coleus has blue flowers in summer with red, green and yellow leaves. Varieties of this tropical plant grow from 25 centimetres to 1 metre high. They are short-lived perennials, which are usually grown as annuals.

**Sweet William, see *Dianthus barbatus***

**Toadflax, see *Linaria vulgaris***

## *Tropaeolum* spp. (nasturtium)

The nasturtium is a low perennial which spreads well and demands moist, and preferably cool, conditions. It has distinctive green oval or heart-shaped leaves, which are edible, and small white, orange or red flowers.

## *Verbena* spp.

The genus Verbena contains plants of quite a variety of sizes, shapes and colours. The common feature of Verbena is that most types have smallish, tubular flowers that appear in summer. These can be pink, red, white, lilac or purple. Some are annual, some are perennial. *Verbena officinalis* was used by early settlers to treat fevers and wounds.

## *Viola* x *wittrockiana* cultivars (pansy)

Pansies are small annuals with beautiful flowers which look wonderful in cottage gardens. Although they do not spread far themselves, they tend to self-propagate readily by dropping seeds.

The long-spurred pansy (*V. calcarata*) has violet or yellow flowers in summer, while heartsease (*V. tricolor*) has flowers of yellow, blue and violet. Pansies prefer rich, moist soils and sunshine, although they don't like hot weather or humidity.

# VEGETABLES

If you can find space for a vegetable garden in your yard, you won't regret it. In some ways, vegetables take a little more work than other parts of the garden. You need to be more thorough with pest control, and many tender young vegies need careful watering early.

But the pleasures of eating a cabbage, cos lettuce or tomato fresh from your garden far outweigh the time and energy involved. As well, and fortunately for asthma and hayfever sufferers, vegetables cause few pollen problems.

You should avoid English spinach (*Spinacia oleracea*) and sweet corn, as they both produce a lot of pollen. Some people might get rashes from the hairier types of tomato plants. And some people will find that root crops can be rough on their skin.

But otherwise, vegetables are a lovely addition to a low allergy garden.

# CHAPTER 8
# SHRUBS

Shrubs are the middle children of the garden – adaptable, hardy and often neglected. They are used to fill the gaps in the garden, just as middle children sit at the table where the eldest won't sit and the youngest can't.

Still, there are many striking shrubs with unusual leaves, colours, flowers and shapes. You need them in your garden. The tighter leaved shrubs are also required if you are to attract small birds to your garden. They need to hide in shrubs to get away from predator birds.

There's a point worth noting if you are planting a native garden with a variety of Australasian trees and shrubs. Most natives don't like having roots disturbed. So digging the soil around your shrubs is not just unnecessary, but it can actually endanger your plants.

So if you have a native garden, there is no need to feel guilty about not digging it. You can tell yourself you are actively protecting the roots. Benign neglect is the way to go.

*Camellia japonica (camellia)*

# Shrubs to choose

## Abelia x grandiflora (glossy Abelia)

This medium-sized shrub is rather uninspiring. It has small green leaves with a tinge of purple and small white flowers in summer and autumn. It is popular in so many gardens because it stands up to the assaults of children with cricket balls, cricket bats and other assorted weapons. In the backyard where I grew up, we had a glossy Abelia behind the stumps, and it used to eat at least one ball each week.

## Azalea, see Rhododendron cultivars

## Baeckia virgata (twiggy heath myrtle)

Indigenous to eastern Australia, this 2 to 3 metre evergreen shrub has thin willowy branches and profuse clusters of white flowers in summer. Its leaves have been brewed to make tea, which is said to be a mild sedative and pleasant to drink.

## Banksia spp.

Banksias are tough evergreen plants requiring little water. They can grow in poor soils, can withstand frosts and droughts, and provide those striking flowers for long periods. There are species of Banksias of all shapes and sizes, and there are species that flower in different colours and in different seasons.

Heath Banksia (B. ericifolia) is a native of New South Wales. It prefers the coast, where it grows to about 4 metres tall. It has 40 centimetre long golden flowers in spring.

Honeysuckle Banksia (B. spinulosa) is a large hardy shrub with cylindrical, 18 centimetre flowers in summer and autumn.

## Bauera rubioides (river rose)

Native to most of Australia, the river rose can grow to 60 centimetres high and 2 metres wide. It has scraggly stems, but small pretty white or pink flowers in summer. It doesn't like drought and prefers protection from the wind.

### *Bauhinia acuminata* (orchid tree)

The orchid tree is a somewhat delicate medium-sized evergreen shrub that needs to be protected from the wind, the frost and the drought. It has white, orchid-like flowers on bare stems at the end of winter and into spring.

### *Boronia heterophylla* (red Boronia)

The red boronia, a native of Western Australia, is a largish evergreen shrub with profuse, red or brown, bell-shaped, highly perfumed flowers appearing from winter to spring. It prefers moist soils and likes to be protected from the wind and from the full sun.

## Bottlebrush, see *Callistemon* spp.

## Bracelet honey myrtle, see *Melaleuca armillaris*

## Californian lilac, see *Ceanothus cyaneus*

### *Callistemon* spp. (bottlebrush)

The many varieties of bottlebrush are all suitable for a low allergy garden, and many of them are beautiful too. They all have the familiar bottlebrush flowers, although the colours vary from whites to yellows to the familiar deep reds. You can get them in sizes ranging from smallish shrubs to medium-sized trees.

Some species, such as the lemon-scented bottlebrush (*C. citrinus*), can have the red spikes all year round, while others flower only in summer. You can even get varieties with yellow or green flowers.

*C. comboynensis*, the Comboyne bottlebrush, has a straight stem and weeping branches. Unlike many natives, bottlebrushes generally prefer a fair bit of water.

### *Camellia* spp.

Camellias are natives of the forests of Japan and China. The leaves have been used traditionally to make a weak tea, and the seed oil was used for lighting, lubrication, cooking and as a cosmetic.

*C. japonica* is a medium to large shrub with large glossy leaves. It prefers a slightly protected position, but is tough when established. It flowers from late autumn through to mid-spring.

*C. sasanqua* is a small tree which flowers in autumn and early winter. It is extremely tough, and can withstand sun, wind and salt, as long as it receives enough water while not flowering. It's hard to pick the flowers, as they tend to fall to bits.

If you plant one of each species, you will have Camellias flowering for six months of the year. You will probably get better results if you pull off some of the buds before they open.

Camellias are favourites in gardens throughout the world. They like rich, well-drained soil with a good covering of leaf debris, which they usually provide themselves.

## *Ceanothus cyaneus* (Californian lilac)
This medium-sized evergreen shrub has dark green leaves and clusters of lilac or cornflower blue flowers in spring and in autumn. It likes the sun, as do all Californians, and is fairly hardy, although it dislikes humidity and is prone to dieback or sudden death in humid climes.

## Coastal rosemary, see *Westringia fruticosa*

## *Correa alba* (white correa)
This is an evergreen shrub which grows to about 1.5 metres high by 1 metre wide with soft, grey-green woolly leaves and white, fuchsia-like flowers from winter through to spring. It is quite striking and grows well in most positions. It even tolerates salty soils.

## *Cotoneaster conspicuus 'Decorus'* (Cotoneaster)
This native of Tibet is an evergreen shrub with brilliant red berries and smallish white flowers. It grows to 2 metres tall and is quite hardy. In Australia there is a move on to discourage Cotoneasters, as birds tend to spread the berries through native bushland and national parks, where the plants are considered a pest.

### *Epacris impressa* (common white heath)

This is an unusual evergreen bush, having tubular pink, red or white flowers hanging down directly off the stems in winter. It is fairly hardy.

### *Escallonia macrantha* (Escallonia)

A large Chilean evergreen shrub with large, glossy, deep green leaves and small, bright pink bell-shaped flowers in spring and summer.

### *Gardenia augusta* cultivars (Gardenia)

The Gardenia is well known for the strong, sweet fragrance of its white bell-shaped flowers. It flowers for up to six months of the year, although it is prone to dropping leaves and flowers. Gardenias tend to last five or six years only before dwindling away or dying suddenly.

While most are compact bushes up to 1.5 metres or so, there is a dwarf variety, *G. augusta 'radicans'*, which is ideal for rockeries, low containers or planting under larger shrubs and trees.

### Glossy Abelia, see *Abelia* x *grandiflora*

### Guinea flower, see *Hibbertia* spp.

### *Hakea* spp.

There are far too many species of Hakea to name, but most of them are native to Western Australia. They are medium-sized evergreen shrubs with fairly distinctive long green-grey leaves, and they enjoy that state's well-drained soils and dry conditions. Many have flowers that are a bit bulbous and spiky.

The pincushion plant (*H. laurina*) grows to about 4 metres and, in autumn, has profuse pink and cream flowers which look like pincushions, if you use your imagination.

The willow-leaved Hakea (*H. salicifolia* or *H. saligna*) has small white flowers in spring and summer.

Refer also to Chapter 16, as the leaves of this species can irritate the skin.

## *Hibbertia* spp. (guinea flower)

The guinea flower, native to Australia not Guinea (it is named after the unit of currency), is a rather ordinary shrub with open yellow flowers in summer.

*H. scandens* is an excellent groundcover, widely used by landscape architects because of its adaptability.

## *Kunzea affinis* (Kunzea)

The Kunzea, a native of Western Australia, is a medium-sized evergreen shrub with fluffy pink flowers in spring.

## *Lavandula dentata* (French lavender)

This sweet-smelling shrub grows easily to a metre high and wide. It has tiny green-grey leaves and deep lavender flowers appearing in autumn and spring. It can be used crushed to scent bathrooms or wardrobes.

## *Leptospermum lanigerum* v. *macrocarpum* (silky tea tree)

Even though it's called a tree, this plant is more of a large shrub with smallish white flowers appearing along the branches in summer.

## *Melaleuca armillaris* (bracelet honey myrtle)

This large evergreen shrub has papery bark, bright green spiky leaves and creamy bottlebrush-like flowers in spring. It is quite hardy and prefers plenty of sun.

## *Plumbago auriculata* (Plumbago)

The Plumbago is a medium-sized South African shrub with masses of sky-blue flowers in summer and autumn. It can look a bit straggly if untouched, but bushes up well if pruned hard after flowering. It can be trained to grow up against a wall or a trellis, although its not a true climber. Perhaps it could be called a scrambler.

A white variety is also available, and recently the 'Royal Cape' became available, which is a smaller variety with a deeper blue flower.

## *Rhododendron* cultivars (azaleas)

People write whole books about azaleas, but basically the ones most commonly grown in Australia and New Zealand are small to medium-sized evergreen shrubs from Japan and China that produce spring flowers in a huge range of colours. They are quite fragile. They prefer broken or dappled light, acid soils, and are susceptible to the lace bug. You shouldn't water them from above, as they are prone to petal blight. The smaller azaleas are quite precious, growing best in pots, but the larger ones survive anywhere, even if they don't prosper.

They'll take the full sun that some other plants can't handle. One thing to be wary of; the leaves of azaleas are poisonous.

## *Rhododendron* spp. (Rhododendron)

Various species of Rhododendron exist, ranging from small shrubs to good-sized trees. They all have long dark green leaves and largish, impressive light-coloured flowers in spring. Some of them are quite fragrant. Most prefer cool climates and acid soil.

## River rose, see *Bauera rubioides*

## *Salvia* spp.

The genus Salvia contains plants ranging from small annual herbs to large evergreen shrubs. There are more than one hundred and eighty species of Salvia grown in Australia and New Zealand, and a large number of cultivars. They have distinctive lipped flowers of a variety of colours, and they prefer drier soils and open, sunny positions.

Some varieties of Salvia are annuals, offering red, white and blue flowers.

## Snowball, Guelder rose, see *Viburnum opulus*

## *Streptosolen jamesonii* (marmalade bush)

This large Colombian shrub is also known as the fire bush or the orange Browallia. 'Ginger Meggs' is a trade name given to one particular type of marmalade bush. It is a little like the Plumbago, except the flowers are orange.

**Twiggy heath myrtle, see (*Baeckia virgata*)**

## *Viburnum opulus* (snowball, Guelder rose)
This 3 metre tall deciduous shrub has clusters of white flowers early in summer. It likes the sun, but needs moisture.

## *Weigela florida* (Weigela)
The Weigela is a striking large deciduous shrub with rose-coloured, trumpet-shaped flowers and open leaves. It prefers rich soils in a sunny position, but won't stand drying out.

## *Westringia fruticosa* (coastal rosemary)
This evergreen shrub has green-grey leathery leaves and white flowers, spotted with purple, in summer. It grows to about a metre high, but can spread widely.

# CHAPTER 9
# TREES

Most of us inherit gardens with trees. In the average suburban backyard, there are two down against the back fence, and maybe one against the side where the prevailing wind comes from. And if you move into a house with a pool, there will be a deciduous tree hanging over it. So for most of us, there's not a lot you can do about trees except pull them up and replace them. If you're lucky, you get to plant one or two, but you have to choose carefully if space is limited.

If you live on a bit more land, or have moved into a new house with gardens to create from scratch, there is more scope to play with trees. If you're in this situation, you're lucky. You'll be able to create shade, create height, create havens for birds, create playrooms for kids and create a feeling of depth and perspective.

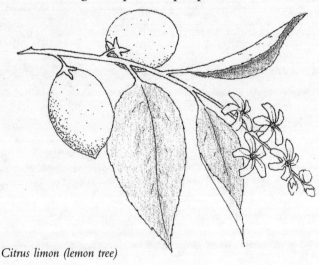

*Citrus limon (lemon tree)*

# Trees to choose

## *Acmena centimetreena smithii, Syzyium* spp. (lillypilly)

The lillypilly is a medium-sized tree, native to the east coast of Australia, which likes a protected shady position. Lillypillies have deep green leaves and fluffy white or cream flowers in summer. The fruit can be eaten, although it can be very tart, and can be made into a jam, where all that sugar dilutes the taste.

## *Agonis flexuosa* (peppermint tree)

A native of Western Australia, but now growing throughout Australia and New Zealand, the peppermint tree is a small, heavily scented tree that looks a little like a willow. It has numerous small white flowers in spring, and responds well to pruning.

## *Agonis marginata* (willow myrtle)

The willow myrtle is really a smaller version of the peppermint tree, growing to 3 metres instead of 15 metres. Its leaves don't smell as strongly as do those of the peppermint tree.

## *Araucaria heterophylla* (Norfolk Island pine)

This huge, beautiful, slow-growing, evergreen tree is popular throughout Australia wherever it can be grown. It reaches more than 50 metres high and spreads far and wide. For this, you need a yard more than a garden. Or, better still, land.

Norfolk pines have a reputation for being a little temperamental. Some of the lines of pines along Sydney's beaches have died, said to have occurred because of pollution.

## *Banksia integrifolia* (coast Banksia or white honeysuckle Banksia)

This is an evergreen tree which may grow up to 15 metres tall. It has a stunted trunk, twisted, gnarled branches, long irregular leaves and lime-yellow spiky flowers.

## *Banksia serrata* (old man Banksia)

Also known as the red honeysuckle Banksia or the saw Banksia, this Banksia is a medium-sized tree with long, harsh, leathery leaves and grey, woolly spikes of flowers in summer.

## Cabbage tree palm, see *Livistona australis*

## *Carica papaya* (paw paw)

The paw paw is a tropical evergreen tree, requiring warm, moist, humus-rich soil.

In the past you needed a male tree and a female tree to get fruit. The male flowers are 1 metre long and rather phallic, while the female flowers are more labial. These trees grow to about 8 metres tall. Now, bisexual paw paws are available, and they grow to only about 3 metres. That's handy, because it means you can actually reach the fruit.

The fruit can be huge, and are totally delectable. They appear in summer, and can be carried on the trees for several seasons.

See Chapter 16 for further details of this tree, as the sap may be an irritant.

## Citrus trees

Citrus trees are medium-sized evergreen trees which are fairly easy to grow in most parts of Australia and New Zealand. They need plenty of sun and a fair bit of water. They vary in size from potted varieties for terraces to 10-metre high grapefruits which need a good bit of space to stretch in.

The main Citrus trees are the lemon (*Citrus limon*), orange (*C. aurantium, C. sinensis*), lime (*C. aurantiifolia*) and grapefruit (*C.* x *paradisi*).

## *Eucalyptus ficifolia* (scarlet flowering gum)

This is a rather temperamental smaller tree from the south-western corner of Australia. It has a twisted trunk, rough dark bark and scarlet flowers in summer. It is not all that keen on frost, wind, drought, humidity, sandy soils, or the eastern states or New Zealand.

## *Eucalyptus haemastoma* (scribbly gum)

The scribbly gum is a striking Eucalypt. It has a pale grey or white twisted trunk with scribble marks, which are caused by the larvae of a moth. Flowers are white, and appear from spring to autumn.

## *Eucalyptus nicholii* (peppermint gum)

This is a graceful gum which grows to about 12 metres tall, with white creamy flowers in autumn. The name arises because it has oily peppermint-scented leaves.

## *Ginkgo biloba* (maidenhair tree)

This Chinese native is a deciduous tree which grows to 40 metres or so and spreads wide, so you need a fair space to even consider planting it. It has a thick trunk with reddish bark and unusual leaves.

See Chapter 16, however, as this tree may irritate the skin.

## *Grevillea robusta* (silky oak)

This unusual tree can be either evergreen or deciduous, and grows to a height of 40 metres with a straight trunk and long dark narrow leaves. Its flowers are bright orange-yellow and so full of nectar that you can shake it out.

## *Howea forsteriana* (kentia palm)

The kentia palm is a striking native of Norfolk Island and Lord Howe Island, although it has adapted well to sub-tropical parts of Australia and New Zealand. It is a feather palm, and can grow to 20 metres tall in northern Australia. Further south, it often stays a more manageable 5 metres tall or so.

The kentia palm is extremely adaptable, growing only metres from the shore in its native habitat.

## *Laurus nobilis* (sweet bay, Grecian laurel)

This evergreen tree from Greece has large glossy leaves, black glossy berries and cream flowers. It grows to about 10 metres and prefers a sunny position. It is extremely tough and adaptable, surviving neglect and poor conditions.

Lillypilly, see *Acmena centimetreena smithii*,
*Syzyium* spp.

## *Livistona australis* (cabbage tree palm)

This native of the east coast of Australia is a large palm with more useful parts than most trees. Its 'cabbages' have been boiled and eaten, and its fronds can be woven to make hats. It has plenty of white fragrant flowers early in summer, and prefers plenty of water.

## *Magnolia grandiflora* (Magnolia)

The Magnolia is a graceful, stately tree which has become a favourite of Australasian gardeners.

*M. grandiflora* is evergreen, although most species are deciduous. Large fragrant flowers appear in spring or summer. Magnolias prefer well-composted soil and sunny, well-protected positions.

## *Malus floribunda* (Japanese flowering crab apple)

This small deciduous tree has masses of red buds, which open to paler flowers along the branches in late spring. It has a few tiny bitter apples the size of cherries. It likes a sunny spot in a cool climate.

## *Melaleuca hypericifolia* (red flowering paperbark)

An evergreen, spreading small tree with a smooth straight trunk and large orange-red summer flowers that look a little like bottlebrushes. It grows to about 3 metres high, and doesn't like the frost. Native to Queensland and New South Wales.

## *Melaleuca quinquenervia* (broad-leaved paperbark)

This Melaleuca has a straight trunk with spongy white bark and twisted branches. It has cream bottlebrush-like flowers in spring and summer, and grows to 12 metres high. It likes water, so be careful of pipes, sewers, drains and so on.

## *Nyssa sylvatica* (tupelo)

A deciduous tree which grows to 10 metres, the tupelo comes from the east coast of North America. It has small purplish berries and clusters of white flowers. If grown in moist, rich, loamy soils, its large green leaves change colour beautifully in autumn.

## Orchid tree, see *Bauhinia acuminata*

## *Prunus* spp.

Prunus are very popular small deciduous trees in many parts of Australia. Most have interesting leaf colour changes, and most have small but impressive flowers which give good shows in spring or summer.

The flowering almond *(P. triloba)*, flowering apricot (*P. armeniaca*) and flowering cherry (*P. serrulata* cultivars) are all known to be low in airborne pollen.

---

### WHAT CAN I USE FOR A WINDBREAK?

Many of the trees people like to use for windbreaks, such as cypress pines *(Cupressus spp.)* and poplars, are no good for allergy sufferers. The cypress pines, in particular, produce huge amounts of allergenic pollen.

But if you want a windbreak, you are not restricted to just those plants. You could go for the Pinus species, which produce a low allergen pollen. Radiata pine (*P. radiata*), Aleppo pine (*P. halepensis*) and slash pine (*P. elliottii*) are all suitable. The Canary Island pine *(P. canariensis)* is suitable in cooler climes.

Also eucalypts may be suitable, especially the cooler climate ones such as the snow gum (*Eucalyptus pauciflora*) or the black sallee (*E. stellulata*).

If you need a lower windbreak, then try the larger varieties of bottlebrush (*Callistemon* spp.), *Banksia* spp., the Western Australian peppermint (*Agonis flexuosa*) and the paperbarks (*Melaleuca* spp.).

---

# CHAPTER 10
# GRASSES

Most of us like a lawn, and for good reasons. It's hard to play ball games among shrubs, and it's hard to lie on concrete. Lawns are traditional, attractive and useful.

But unfortunately, most lawns are highly allergenic. If you suffer from hayfever or asthma, the chances are fairly high that your lawn will make it worse. Grasses flower, as do other plants, and most of them give off tonnes of pollen, and most of that pollen is highly allergenic.

It is possible to have a garden without lawn. The Japanese, admittedly a bit cramped for space in many cases, use pebbles instead. Other people use pavers, bricks or a ground cover of chipbark to cover the space we usually reserve for grass.

But if you suffer from grasses, and desperately want a lawn, there are ways you can do it. You can have a more traditional lawn from either buffalo or 'Greenlees Park' couch. Note that most couches produce plenty of pollen and can be quite allergenic – it is only this variety that produces little pollen.

The other way to go is to get into Australian native grasses. These won't produce the same matt finish that you get with a traditional lawn, but you can get quite a nice appearance of a longish, slightly tufty, grassed area.

The only real problem with Australian native grasses is that, as yet, they are not available commercially as turf. So you either have to sow the seeds, or to plant individual grass plants.

The easiest way to plant Australian native grasses is with Enviro-cells, which are small containers resembling something like an upside down pyramid. You plant an Enviro-cell by digging or drilling a hole 25 millimetres wide and 50 millimetres deep. Drop a bit of fertiliser in the hole, then drop the Enviro-cell in, and place mulch around.

These give you a headstart of six to twelve months over seeds, and they mean the grass is more likely to survive.

Enviro-cells are not too bad if you have a small area to grass, but it would be hard work if you had a large block of land that you wanted to plant with grass.

## ALTERNATIVES TO LAWN

There are ways you can have greenery on your ground, and not have a lawn. Some people, especially those with smaller yards, lay inexpensive paving stones in a regular pattern, then plant low-growing perennials between the stones. If you can choose the right plant, you end up with a low maintenance paved effect with some greenery. In the right situation, it looks good.

# Lawn grasses to use

### *Cynodon dactylon* cultivar ('Greenlees Park' couch)

'Greenlees Park' couch is a reasonably hardy introduced grass, although like all couches it tends to go brown in winter and is scared of frosts. It spreads by runners and has few flowers.

### *Microlaena stipoides* (rice grass or weeping grass)

This is an evergreen grass which is good for damp or shady areas. It doesn't grow very tall, making it perfect for use as a natural lawn beneath trees and shrubs. It is too expensive yet for use on a large lawn, but the price will drop with time.

### *Stenotaphrum secundatum* (buffalo grass)

This is a tough, practical introduced grass which produces little pollen. It is hardy, spreads by runners and is easy on people with asthma and hayfever.

The only problem with buffalo is that some people get itchy when they sit on it. But for most, that's a minor problem.

### *Themeda triandra* (kangaroo grass)

Kangaroo grass grows in tufts, rather than spreading by runners. It can be slashed a couple of times a year to 60 centimetres high, but it can't be mown easily.

Kangaroo grass is native to all states of Australia. It grows in all soils, is resistant to drought and humidity. It doesn't mind the cold, but it goes brown in frosts. It is clumpier than your standard lawn, so doesn't look all that good cut short. If left alone, it grows to 1.2 metres, which is a good child-losing height.

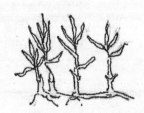

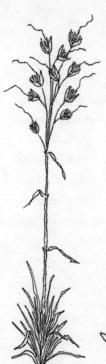

*Themeda triandra*
*(kangaroo grass)*

*Stenotaphrum*
*secundatum*
*(buffalo grass)*

*Cynodon dactylon*
*cultivar*
*('Greenlees Park')*

*Microlaena stipoides*
*(rice grass)*

## WHERE DO YOU GET IT?

Australian native grasses are available in Enviro-cells from:

* New South Wales    AA Bulk (02) 4577 5912
* Victoria    Alliance Seeds (03) 9761 0906
* South Australia    Horley Turf (08) 8383 7015
    Paul Munn (08) 8298 6555
* Queensland    Coomera River Nurseries
    (07) 7573 2077

# Minimising the problems
# from other grasses

Most of us don't have the luxury (or pain) of planting new lawns, so we make do with what we have. If you have a standard pollen-producing lawn, there are ways that you can minimise the problems they cause you.

Grasses release their pollens at certain times of the day. Most do so a couple of hours after sunrise, while a few do so in the middle of the day or in the late afternoon. The pollen rises and sits in a layer 50 centimetres to 2 metres off the ground, drifting on the breeze.

But if you can get out there before the pollen rises off the grass, then you will breathe in less and be likely to suffer fewer problems.

**Mow** while the dew is still on the lawn.
**Garden** while the dew is still on the lawn.
**Mow** as often as you need to so as to stop the lawn flowering and producing pollen.
**Wear a mask** if you are going to use a brushcutter.

Better still, hand on the job of mowing to someone else, if possible.

# Pasture grasses

Pasture grasses like rye-grass (*Lolium perenne*), Kentucky blue grass (*Poa pratensis*), cocksfoot (*Dactylis glomerata*), canary grass (*Phalaris aquatica*) and Timothy grass (*Phleum pratense*) all produce tonnes of pollen, and all are allergenic.

There's not much known about the allergenicity of Australian and New Zealand native pasture grasses, but based on an examination of their structure, the experts believe they are likely to produce far less pollen than the above introduced grasses.

# CHAPTER 11
# GROUND COVER

There are plenty of reasons why, if you want a low allergy garden, you should consider using plenty of ground covers.

One is that if you use ground covers, you have fewer weeds. That, in itself, reduces the load of pollen and irritants in the garden. As well as that, there is less mess and less work.

The second is that if you use ground cover well, you may be able to get away without mulching. As we will explain in Chapter 18, the decision on whether or not to mulch is tricky. It's hard to have a good garden without mulch, but it's hard to imagine avoiding all the moulds and spores and dust that mulch carries. There are ways to use mulch and compost well, and that is probably the best way to go. But if you want to avoid mulching altogether, then plentiful ground cover is the only alternative.

A third reason for going for ground cover is that, if you can do it well, you can reduce the size of your lawn. This means less pollen, less mowing and less work. Many people sick of mowing have got rid of their front lawn and planted it out, relying on ground covers to spread and reduce the amount of work involved. And it comes out well, too.

A fourth reason is that they can look good. There is enough variety in spreading plants to be able to develop a good-looking low garden, then have plants of different heights and shapes to provide the change in texture.

A fifth reason, and a good one for most people, is that a garden full of ground cover requires less water than one with bare soil.

# Ground covers to choose

## *Baeckia ramosissima* (rosy heath myrtle)

This is an evergreen shrub which grows to about 50 centimetres high and wide, although its stems sometimes fall along the ground. It has sparse narrow leaves and scattered pink or white petals which appear in winter, spring or summer. It is quite hardy, and prefers full sun.

## *Campanula* spp. (Canterbury bells)

Canterbury bells are small bushes with spikes of blue, white or pink bell-shaped flowers. Most are perennials, although there are some annual varieties. Some prefer cold climes, while others prefer warmth. They can handle shaded areas, and make excellent ground cover.

## *Cerastium tomentosum* (Snow-in-summer)

This low-growing, creeping perennial has silver-grey leaves and large cup-shaped white flowers – guess when? It needs plenty of sun, and doesn't like drought, humidity or overwatering.

## *Cotula filicula*

The *Encyclopaedia Botanica* makes this plant sound quite menacing, describing its stem as 'stout, creeping, fleshy and hairy'. It sounds more like a tarantula than a small perennial with harmless yellow flowers in summer.

## *Dichondra repens* (kidney weed)

This unattractive-sounding plant does look a little like a weed. It spreads easily, it is tough and its flowers are green and hard to see. Still, it covers the ground.

## *Juniperus* spp.

Junipers, which come from the cypress family, are most commonly trees 10, 20 or 30 metres high. They are used as windbreaks on farms, doubling up as homes for treehouses with their flat well-spread branches. But some junipers are low flat shrubs that make ideal ground cover, especially if the deep green of their leaves is contrasted with the deep greys and sandy colours of natural rock.

Examples of this are the Japanese shore juniper (*J. conferta*) and the creeping juniper (*J. horizontalis*), both of which stay low and grow to a width or 2 metres or more.

Junipers need a fair bit of sun, but not all that much water.

## *Leptospermum* spp. (tea tree)

There are too many varieties of tea tree to go through them all. The common feature is that most varieties have five-petalled white flowers in spring or summer. They are reasonably hardy, although some types need quite a bit of water, and most of them don't like the cold. Most are medium-sized shrubs, up to 5 metres high or so, although there are some spreading types which make suitable ground cover.

*L. rotundifolium* is one squat version that can be used as ground cover. No more than a metre tall, it grows well along the eastern coast of Australia and in New Zealand. It has dark green leaves and large pink flowers with green centres – quite striking.

## *Mazus pumilio*

A low spreading perennial with large, dark green leaves and small tubular lilac flowers in summer. It prefers sunshine and plenty of water. Native to most of eastern Australia, it grows from Queensland to Tasmania. Propagate by dividing it in winter.

## *Mentha diemenica*

A small perennial mint with strongly perfumed leaves and mauve flowers. *Encyclopaedia Botanica* says the leaves were used by the Australian Aborigines to treat menstrual disorders and stomach cramps. It may be hard to find in nurseries.

## *Micromyrtus ciliata* (fringed heath myrtle)

This is an evergreen shrub which grows only 10 to 15 centimetres high, but spreads well into a dense plant, which should keep the weeds at bay. It has tiny deep green leaves and plenty of white bell-shaped flowers in spring which tend to turn pink in summer.

## *Rosmarinus officinalis* 'Prostratus' (rosemary)

Rosemary is a mid-sized shrub which grows in most places, but prefers sun, protection from the wind and well-drained soils. It has dark green leaves with a distinctive aroma, and small blue or white flowers in spring. *R. officinalis* 'Prostratus' makes a lovely ground cover.

## *Thymus* spp. (thyme)

There are quite a few species of thyme, which comes from southern Europe. All are small hardy perennials.

The most common variety in Australia and New Zealand is garden thyme (*T. vulgaris*), which is used as a herb.

## *Vinca major* 'Variegata' (variegated periwinkle)

Periwinkle is a creeping groundcover with glossy variegated leaves and large purple flowers – an attractive combination. It stands up well to dry conditions.

## *Viola hederacea* (native violet)

Native violet is a low spreading plant with rounded leaves and delicate lilac and white flowers mainly in spring, but sometimes at other times of the year. It can be divided in winter, or it will probably just spread quite well on its own. It tends to get a bit close to the stems of other plants, so needs to be kept under control.

---

### SILVER-LEAVED PLANTS

As a general rule, plants with silvery leaves need at least four hours of direct sun each day.

---

# CHAPTER 12
# CLIMBERS

Climbers add variety to a garden. They provide height and they usually provide colour, as many climbers have bright-coloured flowers.

Also, climbers are good at hiding the nasty bits of a garden. Large cement block walls, old toilets, new paling fences, aluminium sheds and neighbours' ugly unpainted garages can all be spruced up or hidden completely by the judicious users of climbers.

Climbers can be used as an alternative to hedges, which are not good for people with allergies, as they collect moulds, spores and dust. Other plants do that, too, but hedges are very dense and need to be trimmed regularly, which stirs everything up.

If you are thinking of a hedge, there's no need to stick to the traditional idea of a green bushy free-standing plant.

Why not stand some lattice or even a simple wire fence and plant a couple of quick-growing climbers? Things may not look good for a year or so, but productive climbers can usually reach a couple of metres high within the first year, then thicken quickly after that.

Climbers can also be used in the open garden. You can buy thin wire trellises that arch over paths or that stand freely in a garden bed.

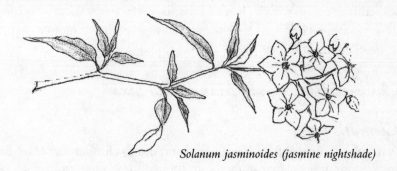

*Solanum jasminoides (jasmine nightshade)*

# Climbers to choose

### *Actinidia deliciosa* (kiwi fruit, Chinese gooseberry)

The Kiwi fruit, which is actually a native of China, comes from a deciduous vine with blotchy oval leaves and fragrant, white, cup-shaped flowers. We all know the fruit – those green/brown hairy berries which can be eaten either with dessert, or just peeled and sliced. Kiwi fruit require cooler climates, protection from the wind and plenty of sun.

Theoretically, you need one male plant and three female plants to get fruit. However, you can buy grafted plants with both male and female parts.

### *Billardiera scandens* (appleberry)

Indigenous to the east coast of Australia, this hardy evergreen climber has yellow bell-shaped flowers in spring, and 3 centimetre long green-yellow edible berries. It prefers an open sunny position, and can stand drought and frost.

Other suitable species include sweet appleberry (*B. cymosa*), purple appleberry (*B. longiflora*) and silky appleberry (*B. sericophora*). They differ in the colour of the flowers and the look of the fruit, but are just as tough.

### *Campsis grandiflora* (trumpet vine)

A deciduous vine, the trumpet vine has aerial roots, meaning it can harm trees that it covers. It is better to leave the trumpet vine on something inert which it can't damage. It snaps lattice readily. The trumpet vine has 5 centimetre long orange trumpet-shaped flowers, and grows well in full sun with plenty of water.

### Chilean jasmine, see *Mandevilla laxa*

### *Clematis* spp.

A deciduous (usually) or evergreen (sometimes) climber that loves full sun, although it helps if the base of the plant is shaded. Prefers a cool climate. Different varieties offer red, white, blue or pink flowers – all of them impressive.

Honesty (*C. vitalba*) is an evergreen climber with twisted, rope-like stems and the most unusual greenish-white star-shaped flowers which appear in dense masses late in summer. It prefers an open sunny position, and doesn't like clay soils.

Clematis tends to flower along the top of the vine, rather than the sides. So it looks good if you are looking down on it, but can sometimes look ordinary if the top of the vine is well above eye level.

## *Kennedia rubicunda* (dusky coral pea)

A tough, quick-growing climber that has long narrow leaves and produces striking 4 centimetre red pea flowers in spring. An Australian native that can take the cold and doesn't need much water.

## *Mandevilla laxa* (Chilean jasmine)

This deciduous jasmine actually originated in Argentina, not Chile. It is not actually related to the jasmine family at all, but like jasmine, it grows quickly. Unlike true jasmines, it likes a bit of shade. It also has larger flowers than the usual jasmine – 5 centimetres across and trumpet-shaped. These appear in summer.

## *Pandorea pandorana* (wonga wonga vine)

This is an evergreen vine which grows up to 6 metres high. It has a woody stem and creamy flowers in loose clusters at the ends of the stems. It flowers in winter or spring, depending on the climate. The wonga wonga vine thrives in coastal gardens but also grows well in dry areas such as central Australia.

## *Passiflora cinnabarina* (crimson passionflower)

This climber, a native cousin of the passionfruit, is a little tender, but quite beautiful and worth the effort of finding the right spot. It produces striking deep red flowers in spring and edible fruit, although not your standard passionfruit.

To reap these rewards, you need a protected, partially shaded spot with damp soil. The crimson passionflower doesn't like to dry out.

## *Passiflora edulis* (passionfruit)

The passionfruit, a native of Brazil, has become a feature of backyards throughout Australia and New Zealand. Paling fences, trellises, swimming pool fences ... the passionfruit is a quick-growing climber producing those lovely bitter-sweet fruit.

It doesn't like shade, dryness or poor soil. It thrives on well cultivated, compost-enriched soil in a sunny spot. The grafted varieties last much longer.

## *Pelargonium peltatum* (ivy leaf geranium)

A native of South Africa, this evergreen ivy-like vine produces clusters of pink, lavender, white, red or two-tone flowers. It likes sunny positions and well-drained soils.

## *Rosa* spp.

There are thousands of different roses, and many varieties climb. Examples include: the Himalayan musk rose (*R. brunonii*), which has dense clusters of single white flowers; the musk rose (*R. moschata*), which has large fragrant creamy white flowers; the Cherokee rose (*R. x laevigata*), which has pale pink flowers; and *R. sempervirens*, which grows to 10 metres high with white flowers.

The Banksia rose (*R. banksiae*), introduced from China, is a graceful climber with long, thornless curving stems and clustered small white or yellow flowers. It prefers an open sunny position, and grows steadily, rather than quickly. It does not attach to support naturally, so tends to spread fairly widely. If guided initially, it looks beautiful over a pergola or archway.

The dog rose (*R. canina*) is a large tough shrub which grows well against man-made structures such as garages, fences, houses, pergolas and gardeners who stand still for too long. It can get up to 5 metres high, and its wild arching spiky stems wave and wander in the breeze. It is available in red, pink or white flowers that cluster in summer.

The dog rose also has those lovely rosehips that you can dry out and keep as a display on the mantelpiece, beside the photos of your kids, dogs, wedding day, friends and/or parents.

## *Solanum jasminoides* (jasmine nightshade, potato vine)

This is a quick-growing, hardy vine that can be grown just about anywhere. Even in its first season, it produces clusters of small tubular white flowers. It can flower throughout the year, but can become invasive if not pruned.

## *Trachelospermum jasminoides* (star jasmine)

This is an excellent evergreen creeper with strongly perfumed white star-shaped flowers in late spring and early summer. It is hardy and long-living.

# CHAPTER 13
# HERBS

Herbs are a wonderful addition to any garden. They look good, some of them smell good and they can be grown in some of those difficult places where there is not a lot of room. You may need only one plant of half a dozen varieties to supply your needs.

Good cooks know how the addition of fresh herbs to a meal can lift it from the ordinary to the tasty. Salads, meats, vegetables, pies, curries, quiches ... there's almost no food that doesn't benefit from the addition of herbs. Herbs are also used for pot pourri, teas, natural remedies and in a variety of traditional medicines.

On top of this, herbs are low allergen plants. Few create much pollen, and few cause skin troubles. All round, a good idea for a low allergy garden.

In planting herbs, there are two ways to do it. One is to plant a herb garden. This has the advantage of keeping them all together, so you can wander to the patch and pick the two or three you need for the next meal. As well, herbs are said to give strength to each other, so planting together can help.

The alternative is to plant them in different places around the garden mixed in with your flowers and vegetables. Some herbs are said to be natural pesticides, protecting other plants from attack.

You can also grow them in unusual containers to make them even more attractive. Laid out in patterns, sitting in an old wheelbarrow (with drainage holes punched in the base), in rockeries, in wooden grocery boxes, in strawberry pots – herbs lend themselves to imaginative uses.

There are a few general comments you can make about herbs. Those of Mediterranean origin (such as lavender, sage and rosemary) prefer open well-drained soils, full sun and plenty of air movement. Most herbs of Asian origin prefer richly composted damp soils.

# Herbs to choose

## *Allium schoenoprasum* (chives)

The different varieties of chives are all perennials that grow long thin leaves – these are great fresh in salads, in clear soups and with cheese and potato dishes.

Chives are good companions for lettuce, tomatoes and cabbages. They grow well in clumps, and don't mind a bit of shade. Cut them down to 10 centimetres a couple of times in summer, and divide the clumps in winter, leaving about ten bulbs per clump. They grow well in pots.

Until the nineteenth century, chives were said to be an aphrodisiac. There's a story that the Siberians, hearing of the approaching marriage of the approaching Alexander the Great, tried to appease him with a gift of chives.

## *Anethum graveolens* (dill)

A fast-growing annual which must be sown during reasonably warm weather – spring in the south, but any time in the north.

The seeds flavour pickles, onions and gherkins, while the leaves can be added to salads and potatoes.

## *Armoracia rusticana* (horseradish)

Horseradish is a medium-sized perennial with large white flowers in winter. It is a bit ugly, and hard to get rid of as it propagates readily unless you remove all the root.

The root is the edible part, served with meat or fish and as a bitter sauce.

## *Foeniculum vulgare* (fennel)

A tall feathery plant which grows to 2 metres. Fennel grows well in coastal areas and on river banks. It is often planted at the back of a herb garden to screen off a fence and provide a contrast with the size and shape of other herbs.

You can used dried fennel leaves to wrap fish before grilling, or add fresh leaves to salads, sauces and soups.

## *Mentha* (mint)

The many varieties of mint will grow in most places, but they prefer damp soil.

Apple mint (*M. suaveolens*) and spearmint (*M. spicata*) are the varieties traditionally used in mint sauces, while eau-de-cologne mint (*M. pipirata 'Citrata'*) and pennyroyal (*M. pulegium)* are used mainly for their aroma in the garden. Both can be crushed and used to scent baths or bathrooms. Pennyroyal is also said to repel insects if rubbed on the skin.

## *Ocimum basilicum* (basil)

An annual which grows about 60 centimetres high in summer, basil has a distinctive aroma and flavour. It is used with beef, salads, eggs, fish and tomato, also in vinegars.

Sow in spring, then either harvest and dry leaves or pick straight from the garden. The leaves are used to treat indigestion and nausea. Will grow indoors.

A good companion for most plants, repelling flies and mosquitoes. If you don't have flyscreens, grow it on your window sill.

## *Origanum marjorana* (marjoram)

A 30 centimetre high perennial with white-pink flowers which is used to season tomato, cheese and bean dishes.

## *Origanum vulgare* (oregano)

An insect-repelling 50 centimetre high perennial with white-pink flowers and soft green leaves of varying sizes. Used to flavour cheese, tomato, bean, egg and meat dishes. Also used on pizza.

## *Petroselinum crispum* (parsley)

Parsley has been a popular herb since Roman times. It is still handy to wave around salads, omelettes, tomato dishes, cheese dishes and meats, if used sparingly. It grows easily, and can last two years.

## Rosmarinus officinalis (rosemary)

A woody shrub a metre high or so, rosemary is well known as an accompaniment to lamb.

Rub washed and crushed leaves into the outside of the lamb before baking, or cut finely and sprinkle on lamb chops before grilling.

## Salvia officinalis (sage)

A prostrate plant with woolly grey leaves and violet, pink or white flowers. It dislikes humidity.

Traditionally used to flavour and preserve meat dishes and vinegar. It is the main seasoning used to flavour traditional stuffings for poultry.

## Satureja hortensis (summer savory)

A summer-growing annual that grows well in rockeries and provides short term ground cover. May keep the weeds at bay, although it looks a bit weedy itself.

Used most often in fish or veal dishes, or in salads. The Germans call it 'bean herb', and use it that way.

## Thymus vulgaris (thyme)

A low spreading herb which prefers fairly dry soil. Lemon thyme has deep green leaves, while other varieties vary. Thyme is used to flavour various meats and poultry.

---

### INDOOR HERBS?

Herbs are mainly outdoor plants, although they can be grown indoors on a sunny window-sill. If you put them in the centre of your living room, you'll soon have a dried arrangement.

---

# Part III
# PLANTS TO AVOID

Plants to Keep Out of Your Garden •

Plants Which May Cause Contact Dermititis •

Plants Which May Irritate the Skin

# CHAPTER 14
# PLANTS TO KEEP OUT OF YOUR GARDEN

The previous seven chapters have recommended plants that have been shown not to cause allergy problems. This chapter lists all the plants that have been shown to be capable of worsening your asthma or hayfever. These are plants that produce windborne pollens which are allergenic.

You might wonder about some of them. You don't have an ash, but the neighbour does. Is there anything you can do about it?

Fortunately, you don't have to. Most plants produce pollens which fall to the ground quite quickly. Most of the pollen released by a plant hits the ground within a few metres of that plant. It is only on windy days that most pollens travel much further.

So if you can keep these plants out of your garden, you will reduce the load of pollen you are breathing. That may make a difference.

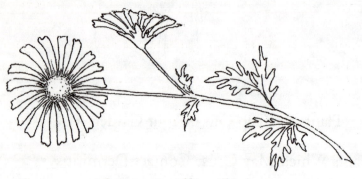

*Osteospermum veldtiana (daisy)*

# Flowers to keep out of your garden

Unfortunately, many of the flowers that we love to use produce allergenic windblown pollens, so they should be avoided by people who are keen to develop a low allergy garden. The main culprits are flowers from the *Asteraceae* family, which includes daisies, Chrysanthemums, Calendulas, Asters and marigolds.

It can be difficult to tell, when buying plants from the nursery, whether flowers belong to this family, as the name *Asteraceae* will not appear on the tag. But the main genera to avoid are Aster, Anthemis, Bellis, Calendula, Chrysanthemum and Tagetes.

Basically, if it has a head that looks anything like a daisy or Chrysanthemum, avoid it.

# Grasses to keep out of your garden

You should avoid all introduced grasses except those named in Chapter 10 – buffalo and 'Greenlees Park' couch. All other introduced grasses produce too much pollen.

# Shrubs and trees to keep out of your garden

## *Acacia* spp. (wattle)

We all known the wattle – evergreen shrubs or trees with beautiful grey-green leaves and striking masses of small rounded yellow flowers. It and other Acacias have a reputation as being highly allergenic. But in a way, wattle's reputation is worse than it need be. When you look at all that sticky heavy yellow stuff lying around the base of the wattle, you think it's pollen. But it's actually the part of the flower that holds the pollen.

Wattle pollen is heavy and sticky, but it is picked up by birds and insects, and transported to other wattles. Most of whatever effect wattle does have probably comes from its perfume, which is strong and may be irritant, rather than its pollen.

## *Acer* spp. (maple)

Some maples have leaves like Liquidambars. They've earned their place in history by being on the Canadian flag, but keep them out of your garden.

## Albizia lophantha

This is a tall Australian shrub, similar to a wattle, now naturalised through most of New Zealand. It produces a lot of pollen, although the pollen is heavy and doesn't move far through the air.

## Alnus spp. (alder)

Alders are medium to large trees, usually deciduous, with straight trunks and smooth or cracked bark. The most common alder, *A. jorullensis*, keeps its leaves in warmer areas.

## Ash, see Fraxinus spp.

## Betula spp. (birch)

Birches are small cool climate trees with white silvery bark which peels off in strips. They have small, light green leaves, and they flower in spring. They grow well near water, and are often planted as specimen trees. Birches have very light pollens which can travel great distances on the wind. They are a common cause of problems. People who are allergic to birches may also be allergic to a variety of fresh fruit and vegetables.

## Brush wattle, see Albizia lophantha

## Casuarina equisetifolia (she-oak)

A large tree found in warmer climes, the she-oak has silvery green needle-like leaves and small cones.

## Coprosma spp.

There's a great variety of Coprosma native to New Zealand, including the common taupata (*C. repens*) and karamu (*C. robusta*) bushes. Most grow 1 to 3 metres high and flower in spring.

## Corylus avellana (hazel)

This is a small tree or large shrub, with branches growing out at an angle from the base. It has heart-shaped leaves, rough hairs and 5 centimetre long yellow catkins. It grows to about 5 metres high, and flowers in late winter or early spring.

## *Cupressus macrocarpa* (Monterey cypress)
A medium-sized cypress with a large billowing crown, which may be as wide as the plant is high.

## *Cupressus sempervirens* (cypress)
The cypress is a pine often grown as an ornamental tree in gardens, or as a windbreak on farms. It has shapely cones and small, sharp deep green leaves. It flowers from late winter through to summer, and produces a lot of pollen.

## Elm, see *Ulmus* spp.

## *Fraxinus* spp. (ash)
The ash is a large solid tree with smooth grey bark and black buds. It does not affect a lot of people, but will make some people's asthma or hayfever worse. It flowers in late spring.

## Hazel, see *Corylus avellana*

## *Juglans* spp. (walnut)
Walnuts are impressive trees with smooth grey bark, large light green leaves and, obviously, walnuts.

## *Ligustrum* spp. (privet)
Privet is a small tree or large shrub with oval leaves, clusters of white flowers and black poisonous berries. People used to plant privet as a hedge, but it has come to be recognised as a noxious weed in Australia and it should be stamped out. Some people suffer quite badly from privet, especially when it flowers in summer.

Privet is fairly easy to remove, but notoriously difficult to eradicate. You can dig it out, but any roots left behind may well shoot to form another tree. Birds spread its seeds readily, so privets keep springing up in areas where they have once been.

It has often been said (well, maybe not, but it should have been said), that the price of ridding your garden of privet is eternal vigilance. That, and putting weedkiller or kerosene on any roots left behind.

## *Liquidambar styraciflua* (Liquidambar)

The Liquidambar is a glorious tree, and it's a terrible shame that it's in this chapter, and not the one on low allergen trees. It grows between 10 metres and 50 metres high, depending on the variety, it has branches running straight from the trunk, which makes it good for climbing, and it has the most gorgeous maple-shaped leaves which go a brilliant orange-red in autumn, before falling. The leaves even look good in mulch. Maybe you could convince a non-allergic friend to plant one, so you could go to visit it some time.

## Maple, see *Acer* spp.

## *Melia azedarach* (white cedar)

This native of Asia and Australia is a stout medium-sized tree with rusty-grey bark, orange berries and impressive clusters of lilac flowers in spring.

## *Morus nigra* (mulberry)

The mulberry is a lovely, smallish tree with large open leaves, delectable fruit and, best of all, silkworms.

Despite their beauty and the pleasure they bring to children, mulberries aren't great trees to have around. Aside from the allergy problem, which can be quite severe for some people, birds eat the berries then drop their purple faeces all over your washing. It's very hard to get the stains out.

## Mulberry, see *Morus nigra*

## Oak, see *Quercus* spp.

## *Olea* spp. (olive)

Olive trees come in a range of sizes and shapes, from 5 metre shrubs to 30 metre trees. The European olive (*O. europaea*) is the one we cultivate to harvest olives. You're better off ducking down the deli to get your olive fix.

## Plane tree, see *Platanus* x *hybrida*

## *Platanus* x *hybrida* (plane tree)

Plane trees are beautiful, tall trees with spreading branches, large bright green maple-like leaves and distinctive round spiky catkins. They are often planted along footpaths, as they overarch well out of reach of cars, and they tolerate pollution and soil compaction well.

Unfortunately, they are quite allergenic, especially in spring when they flower and produce massive amounts of pollen.

## *Populus deltoides* (poplar, cottonwood)

This poplar is a big rangy tree with an open, spreading crown. It is often used as a windbreak.

## Privet, see *Ligustrum* spp.

## *Quercus* spp.

There are more than four hundred species of oak. Most are large and impressive, although a few are small enough to grow in suburban gardens. Most flower in spring.

## *Salix* spp. (willow)

Willows are distinctive trees, the best known of which is the weeping willow. There are a host of willows with unusual names: the Chilean pencil willow, the cricket bat willow, the furry willow, the pussy willow, the woolly willow and the tortured willow. All produce allergenic windborne pollen.

However in Australia and New Zealand, most willows (except the pussy willow) are female, meaning they do not produce pollen.

## *Ulmus* spp. (elm)

Elms are large spreading deciduous trees with a stout trunk which are usually found only in larger gardens. Their light green leaves are heavily striped with serrated edges.

## Walnut, see *Juglans* spp.

**White cedar, see *Melia azedarach***

**Willow, see *Salix* spp.**

# Herbs

## *Anthemis nobilis* (chamomile)

Chamomile is a smallish perennial with white daisy-like flowers. Its leaves are often brewed to make a tea which is drunk, apart from its taste, to treat an upset stomach or a fever.

Unfortunately, chamomile is one of the daisy family, so it falls into that category of producing allergenic windborne pollen.

## *Artemisia absinthium* (wormwood)

Wormwood is a medium-sized perennial with long, silvery, fragrant leaves. It has small round yellow daisy-like flowers gathered in bunches along the branches.

# Weeds

Nobody wants any weeds at all in their garden, on the basis that they are ugly, they are untidy, they crowd out the plants that you want to be there and they create work in trying to get rid of them. But if all weeds are created evil, some are more evil than others.

One of the worst is the genus *Plantago* (plantains), which are found throughout Australia and New Zealand wherever there is lawn, garden or concrete paths. They are highly allergenic for some people, causing serious problems.

Plantains (*Plantago* spp.) are quite distinctive. They have a rosette of heavily ribbed leaves, and a central petalless flower. In some parts of Australia and New Zealand, plantains flower for up to nine months of the year.

To get rid of plantain successfully, you have to either use herbicides or dig under them to get the long single tap root out. If you see them, get rid of them.

The weed pellitory (*Parietaria judaica*), which is also known as 'asthma weed', is another major problem for allergy sufferers. It came from the southern Mediterranean region in the early 1900s, and has spread from the dock at Woolloomooloo throughout Sydney, and then on throughout the coastal cities of eastern Australia. It flowers throughout the year, and seems to be causing increasing problems.

Paterson's Curse (*Echium vulgare*) is a perennial up to 1 metre high, with a hairy erect unbranching stem, bluish green leaves, and rose-pink flowers going blue or purple appear in spring and summer. It took over many pastures in the southern half of Australia spreading from east to west during the 1960s and 1970s, but has gradually become less of a problem with biological control methods. It commonly causes hayfever.

Ragweed (*Ambrosia artemisiifolia*) is a green weed with green flowers, which is spreading down the east coast of Australia from Queensland. Its pollen can cause hayfever and asthma, and the whole plant may cause contact dermatitis. Ragweed is difficult to eradicate.

---

**If it looks like a daisy, it is likely to be allergenic.**
**Don't plant it.**

---

# CHAPTER 15
# PLANTS WHICH MAY CAUSE CONTACT DERMATITIS

Apart from the plants that are capable of causing allergies because of their pollens, there are quite a few plants that cause problems if you touch them.

This chapter contains the names of plants that may cause contact dermatitis. This is a reddening and blistering of the skin which can develop into a serious illness. People with severe contact dermatitis may have a fever, feel nauseous, have swollen glands and generally feel shocking. Occasionally, it is life-threatening.

As a general rule, the plants that cause contact dermatitis are hairy or sticky, and frequently have soft stems. Some have spikes. Others have milky sap, which is usually quite alkaline and bitter.

While it is OK to have these plants in your garden, you shouldn't touch them. If you develop contact dermatitis, you should seek medical attention.

## Plants not to touch

### *Calendula officinalis* (Calendula, pot marigold, English marigold)

The leaves and sap of this popular small annual with open yellow or orange winter flowers may cause allergic reactions such as dermatitis and urticaria.

### *Euphorbia pulcherrima* (poinsettia)

Tall shrubs or smallish trees with striking red and green flowers. They are unforgettable if seen, and a wonderful addition to a garden, but the sap can cause contact dermatitis.

## *Grevillea* spp.

There are Grevilleas that creep and others that soar. The main features in common are the familiar toothbrush flower, their slightly sharp serrated leaves and their ability to cause contact dermatitis. The 'Robyn Gordon' Grevillea, a popular and pretty plant which flowers for long periods, is one of the worst. Others include *G. sericea* and *Grevillea* 'Poorinda Firebrand'.

## *Hedera helix* (common or English ivy)

A tough and fast-growing creeper and climber that goes on to destroy the trees it chokes, the walls it climbs and the fences it smothers. Contact with the leaves, and particularly the stems, can cause dermatitis. Get rid of it, anyway.

## *Helichrysm diosmifolium*

This plant may cause allergic reactions of the skin. It can be severe.

## *Primula* spp. (Primula, polyanthus, primrose)

Any of these flowers can cause contact dermatitis. The leaves have that tell-tale slight hairiness.

## *Toxicodendron succedaneum*, formerly *Rhus succedanea* (Rhus tree)

This glorious ornamental tree, a brilliant orange-red in autumn, is so toxic to so many people that it has been declared a noxious plant in many parts of Australasia. The young hairy growths seem to cause the worst problems.

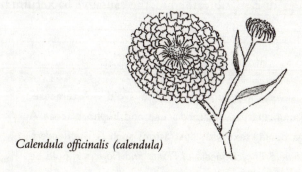

*Calendula officinalis (calendula)*

# CHAPTER 16
# PLANTS WHICH MAY IRRITATE THE SKIN

Apart from those causing dermatitis, there are many plants which can irritate the skin if you touch them.

The bulk of the following list has been derived from material collated by Frances Bodkin, author of *Encyclopaedia Botanica*, in her preparation for a new book on dangerous plants found in Australia. During her research, she spoke to farmers, Aboriginal people and nursery owners, she sorted through doctors' reports and hospital reports, and she gathered information from the universities of Hawaii and Durban, where there has been substantial research done on dangerous plants.

This list is comprehensive, but it shouldn't scare keen gardeners or bushwalkers. It tells what may happen, not what will happen. So if, for example, we say that the sap of agrimony may irritate, that means that it might well irritate some people, but it certainly wouldn't affect everybody.

A few general tips: all gardeners should be careful, and keep their skin covered. This means gardening with hats, gloves, long sleeves, long pants, shoes and 15+ sunscreens. This reduces the chances of sunburn, insect bites, allergic reactions, contact dermatitis, skin infections and poisoning. Although Legionnaires' disease is breathed in, the causative bacterium lives in soils.

## FAMILIES

There are several key family groups to avoid – Asteraceae, Araceae, Ranunculaceae, Anacardiaceae and Euphorbiaceae. A thorough gardening text with illustrations such as *The Readers' Digest Gardeners' Encyclopaedia of Plants and Flowers* should be able to provide common features.

# Plants not to touch

## *Acacia melanoxylon* (black acacia, blackwood)

An evergreen tree to 30 metres with a sturdy trunk, the black acacia has long greyish green leaves, round pale yellow flowers in winter and spring, and long blackish brown pods. The wood may irritate.

## *Achillea millefolium* (milfoil, angel flower, woundwort, yarrow)

A perennial herb to 60 centimetres with long, fine dark green leaves and pink or white daisy-like flowers in summer and autumn. The sap may cause irritation.

## *Aconitum napellus* (Aconite, wolfsbane, monkshood)

A perennial to 1 metre with dark green leaves and dark blue flowers in snapdragon-like spikes in summer. The sap is said to be quite poisonous if it enters an open wound. Any part of the plant can irritate, but especially the rootstock (which is the part that looks like ginger).

## *Agave* spp. (spiked aloe, century plant)

A stout, rosette-forming succulent to 2.5 metres with smooth greyish leaves arising from the base and greenish yellow flowers. Cuts from the spiky leaf tips may cause persistent, painful wounds, and the sap may irritate.

## *Agrimonia eupatoria* (agrimony, salt and pepper)

A small perennial shrub with a straight, hairy stem, long deep green leaves and clusters of small yellow flowers in summer. The sap may irritate.

## *Ailanthus altissima* (tree of heaven)

A large deciduous tree with smooth greyish bark, deep green leaves and dense clusters of yellowish flowers in spring. The pollen may cause hayfever, and the leaves and flowers may irritate.

## *Alisma plantago aquatica* (water plantain)

A perennial water plant to 1 metre with small pale lilac flowers in summer. The tubers may irritate.

## *Allium* spp. (onion, garlic, chives)

Biennial or perennial herbs with hollow erect blue-green leaves arising from the base, and small greenish-white or mauve flowers in spring. The sap may irritate.

## *Alocasia macrorrhiza* (elephant's ear, Cunjevoi)

A robust evergreen perennial to 2 metres with a solid stem like a mature but miniature palm, glossy green leaves like elephant's ears, and red berries on spikes. Any part of the plant may irritate the skin.

## *Amaranthus retroflexus* (red root amaranth)

An annual to 1 metre with long hairy leaves and tiny red flowers on spikes. The pollen causes hayfever, and any part of the plant may irritate.

## American bittersweet, see *Celastrus scandens*

## *Amsinckia* spp. (ironweeds, yellow burweeds, tarweed, fiddlenecks)

Annuals to 1 metre with long heavy leaves, black nutlets and small yellow flowers crowded on one side of a spike. Any part of these plants may irritate the skin.

## *Anacardium occidentalis* (cashew nut)

A medium-sized evergreen tree with leathery leaves and fragrant deep pink tubular flowers in spring. And, of course, the nuts. Unfortunately, the leaves, fruit and sap may all irritate.

## *Anagallis arvensis* (scarlet pimpernel)

A small annual with blue-green leaves and star-shaped scarlet flowers in summer. The leaves may irritate.

## *Ananas comosus* (pineapple)

An evergreen plant to 1.5 metres growing only in the tropics, the pineapple has long spiky leaves growing from the base. The plant's sap may be irritant, and a few people have similar reactions to the skin of the fruit.

### *Anemone nemorosa* (wood anemone)

A perennial plant to 30 centimetres with deep green three-lobed leaves, a slender stem and a large solitary white flower. Any part of the plant may be irritant.

### *Angelica archangelica* (Angelica)

A biennial or perennial plant to 2 metres with a stout stem, bright green leaves and greenish white flowers in spring and autumn. The sap may irritate the skin.

### Angelica tree, see *Aralia spinosa*

### *Annona cherimola* (custard apple)

A small evergreen tree with dull purple flowers in spring and large, yellowish, pulpy fruit. The sap may irritate.

### *Anredera cordifolia* (lamb's tail, Madeira vine, mignonette vine)

A slender, twisting creeper with large heart-shaped leaves and fragrant white flowers on 30 centimetre long spikes. Any parts of this vine may be irritant.

### *Anthemis* spp. (chamomiles)

Chamomiles are small annuals or perennials with dark green leaves and white daisy-like flowers in summer. Any part of the plant may irritate. This includes corn chamomile (*A. arvensis*), stinking chamomile (*A. cotula*) and chamomile (*A. nobilis*).

### *Aralia spinosa* (angelica tree)

A small tree with a stout, prickly stem, profuse white flowers in summer and succulent black berries. The bark may irritate.

### *Arctium lappa* (burdock)

A biennial plant to 1.5 metres with purple tubular flowers in summer. It has heart-shaped leaves with hairs on top, which may cause irritation.

## *Argemone* spp. (Mexican poppy, devil's fig, thistle of Peru)

This small perennial thistle has yellow flowers and long grey-green leaves with spiky edges. If they don't get you, the seeds released from the capsules can irritate.

## *Arisaema* spp. (Indian turnip, bog onion, Jack in the pulpit)

A perennial to 1 metre with huge glossy dark green leaves, red berries and spikes of solitary purple-green leaves in spring. The sap may irritate the skin.

## *Arnica montana* (Leopardbane, mountain tobacco)

A small perennial with long green leaves arising from the base, a hairy stem and orange-yellow daisy-like flowers. Contact with any part of the plant may irritate.

## *Artemisia absinthium* (wormwood, absinthe)

See Chapter 14 for details of the plant. Contact with the flowers and leaves may irritate.

## *Asarum* spp. (wild ginger)

A short fleshy plant with large glossy green leaves, reddish or purple bellshaped flowers in spring and hairy capsules. Any part of the plant may be irritant.

## *Asparagus officinalis* (Asparagus)

Any part of this plant – edible stems, feathery leaves, white flowers or red berries, may irritate the skin.

## Azaleas, see *Rhododendron* spp.

## Banana tree, see *Musa acuminata* cultivars

## *Begonia* spp.

Perennial evergreen plants with flowers of different hues, depending on the species. The large dark green leaves may irritate the skin.

## Bignonia tree, see *Catalpa speciosa*

## Black spear grass, see *Heteropogon contortus*

## Blanket flower, see *Gaillardia* spp.

## Blue cohosh, see *Caulophyllum thalictroides*

## *Borago officinalis* (borage, bugloss)

An annual to 1 metre with a straight hollow stem, large, wrinkled hairy leaves and bright blue star-shaped flowers in summer. The hairs may irritate.

## *Brachyachne* spp. (native couch)

These annual grasses may irritate the skin.

## *Brachychiton* spp. (Kurrajong, bottle tree)

Deciduous or evergreen trees to 30 metres, whose trunks become bottle-shaped with age. They have long green leaves, bell-shaped flowers of red, pink, white, cream or yellowish green, and 12 centimetre long boat-shaped pods containing hairy seeds. The seeds and hair are irritant.

## *Brassica* spp. (mustard)

Large annual or biennial herbs with yellow four-leafed flowers in spring or summer. Contact with any part of the plant may cause dermatitis.

## *Bryonia* spp. (white bryony, tetterberry)

A slender twining vine with prickly tendrils, small green, white or yellow flowers in summer, and small round black berries. The berries, roots and sap may irritate.

## Buckwheat, see *Polygonum fagopyrum*

Burdock, see *Arctium lappa*

Button Grass, see *Dactyloctenium radulans*

Cajuput, see *Melaleuca leucadendra*

## *Calonyction aculeatum* (moonflower)
A slender, woody creeper with heart-shaped leaves and fragrant funnel-shaped flowers which open only at night. Any part of the plant may be highly irritant.

## *Caltha palustris* (Marsh marigold, king cup, water cowslip)
A small perennial with bright green kidney-shaped leaves and large glossy bright yellow flowers. The sap may irritate.

## *Campsis radicans* (trumpet vine)
A deciduous vine with fern-like leaves and large red or orange flowers. The leaves and flowers may irritate.

## *Capsella bursa-pastoris* (shepherd's purse)
A small annual or biennial with 15 centimetre leaves arising from the base, small white flowers and wedge-shaped pods. The seeds in those pods may irritate.

## *Capsicum* spp. (African pepper, cayenne, Capsicum, chili pepper)
Smallish perennial plants with white star-shaped flowers in spring and summer, and those lovely fruit. Unfortunately, the fruit and sap may irritate the skin.

## *Cardiospermum halicacabum* and *C. grandiflorum* (Balloon vine, heart seed, blister creeper)
The sap of these vines, which have large white flowers in spring and balloon-like capsules, may irritate the skin.

## *Carica papaya* (paw paw)

A small tropical tree with a straight, hollow, spongy trunk, huge irregular leaves, yellow funnel-shaped flowers and those gorgeous fruit. The sap may be an irritant.

## *Caryota mitis* (fishtail palm)

An evergreen palm to 5 metres, with 1 to 2 metre long leaves. It has bright red berries and small creamy flowers on spikes. The sap is an irritant.

## Cashew nut, see *Anacardium occidentalis*

## *Cassia* spp. (Senna, coffee Senna, ant bush, pepper leaf Senna, arsenic bush)

These medium-sized evergreen shrubs have long brown pods and buttercup-like flowers. The seeds, leaves and sap may all irritate.

## *Catalpa speciosa* (bignonia tree)

A deciduous tree up to 30 metres tall with heart-shaped hairy leaves, brown oblong pods and white tubular flowers. These flowers may irritate.

## *Caulophyllum thalictroides* (blue cohosh)

A small perennial with dark blue berries and yellowish green flowers in summer. The berries and roots may irritate.

## *Cedrus deodara* (deodar)

A large evergreen with pale green needle-like leaves. The wood, the sap and the cones, which start off violet then turn brown, may all irritate.

## Celandine poppy, greater celandine see *Chelidonium majus*

## *Celastrus scandens* (American bittersweet)

A sturdy deciduous vine with orange berries and masses of yellow-green flowers in spring. The berries may irritate if eaten.

### *Cercis canadensis* (redbud)

A medium sized deciduous tree with greyish bark, heart-shaped leaves and large, rose-pink, pea-shaped flowers in early spring, before the leaves. The sap and the seeds, which are found in large oblong pods, may irritate.

### Chamomiles, see *Anthemis* spp.

### *Chelidonium majus* (celandine poppy)

A small perennial or biennial with a slender stalk, pale green leaves and large bright yellow flowers in summer and autumn. The sap may irritate.

### *Chimaphila umbellata* (pipsissewa)

A low, spreading perennial with glossy dark green leaves, and pink or white flowers with purple centres in spring and summer. The leaves and stems may irritate.

### *Chrysanthemum* spp. (Marguerite, ox-eye daisy, Shasta daisy, feverfew)

The flowers, leaves and stems of these beautiful daisies can all irritate.

### *Cinnamomum zeylandicum* (cinnamon)

A rare medium-sized evergreen tree with pale brown bark, leathery leaves, black berries and small yellow tubular flowers. The sap and the wood may irritate.

### *Clematis* spp. (old man's beard, traveller's joy, headache vine)

Slender, twining deciduous vines with single cream flowers in spring. The leaves and sap may irritate.

### *Cleome* spp. (spider plant, tickweed)

Large annuals with hairy or spiny stems and summer flowers in yellow, orange or pink. The seeds and sap may irritate.

### Cochorus olitorius (jute)

An annual plant to 1.5 metres with a flexible green-brown fibrous stem, long bright green leaves and yellow flowers. The seeds and hairs may irritate.

### Coffea arabica (coffee tree)

A large evergreen shrub with glossy green leaves, white flowers and red berries. The uncooked beans may irritate.

### Colocasia esculentum (taro, dashun, elephant's ears)

A perennial to 1 metre with large dark green leaves shaped like elephant's ears. It has green flowers and red berries. Any part of the plant may irritate.

### Conium maculatum (hemlock, carrot fern)

A biennial plant to 1.5 metres with a hollow stem, dull green serrated leaves and white flowers. Any part of the plant can irritate the skin, while eating the leaves may be fatal.

### Cornus sanguinea (dogwood)

A deciduous shrub to 4 metres with rough bark, reddish brown twigs, bluish black berries and small white flowers in summer. The plant hairs can be terribly irritant.

### Cottonwood, see Populus deltoides

### Crinkle Bush, see Lomatia silaifolia

### Cryptocarya pleurasperma (poison walnut)

A large evergreen tree with grey bark, long narrow leaves and a large round berry containing a nut. The sap and the nut may irritate.

### Cryptostegia grandiflora (rubber vine)

A vigorous evergreen vine with large dark green leaves, trumpet-shaped flowers of white lilac or purple, and woody pods. The leaves, sap and seeds may all irritate the skin.

## *Cucumis* spp. (prickly paddy melon, wild cucumber, paddy melon)

Annual plants which spread to 5 metres with a hairy, tendrilled stem, dark to yellowish green leaves, white flowers and those fruit. The stems and the skin of the fruit may irritate.

## Custard apple, see *Annona cherimola*

## *Cydonia oblonga* (quince)

A medium-sized deciduous tree with white or rose-pink flowers in spring, and the quince fruit. The seeds and the juice of the fruit may be irritating.

## *Cynaria scolymus* (globe artichoke)

A medium-sized perennial shrub with woolly leaves and violet or white funnel-shaped flowers in spring and summer. The flowers may irritate.

## *Cypripedium* spp. (lady's slipper)

These are popular orchids with long ribbed leaves and large yellow and reddish brown flowers in summer. Any part of the plant can be irritant.

## *Dactyloctenium radulans* (button grass)

An annual to 50 centimetres, with dark green leaves and hairs which may irritate.

## *Dalbergia* spp. (Rio rosewood)

An evergreen tree to 20 metres with a short stout trunk, green leaves and white pea-shaped flowers in clusters. The wood may irritate.

## *Danthonia* spp. (wallaby grass)

A perennial grass to 1.5 metres with blue-green leaves.

## *Daubentonia* spp. (Brazilian glory pea, orange locust, wild macaw plant)

Deciduous shrubs to 2.5 metres with orange-red pea-shaped flowers. Any part of these plants may irritate.

## *Davidsonia pruriens* (Queensland itch tree)

An evergreen tree to 12 metres with long elliptical green leaves and 5 centimetre red berries. Contact with the hairs, sap or fruit may irritate and cause hives.

## *Dendrocnide* spp. (stinging tree, Gympie bush, gimpi gimpi)

A large evergreen tree with large heart-shaped leaves and red berries. Any part of the tree may irritate.

## *Derris elliptica* (Derris)

An evergreen vine whose green leaves have a silky undersurface. It has bright red pea-shaped flowers in clusters. The roots may irritate.

## *Dieffenbachia* spp. (dumb cane)

A robust perennial to 2 metres with huge dark green or mottled leaves and white flowers in summer. The stem, leaves and sap may irritate. It earned its name because it was fed to slaves in the USA to render them unable to speak.

## *Dimorphotheca* spp. (South African daisy, white veldt daisy)

Tall daisies with purplish-pink flowers with blue centres. Any part of the plant may irritate the skin.

## Dogwood, see *Cornus sanguinea*

## *Doryphora sassafras* (yellow sassafras, Canary sassafras)

A large evergreen rainforest tree with aromatic wood, fine scaly grey bark, glossy deep green leaves and white star-shaped flowers. Its sap may be irritant.

## *Drosera* spp. (sundew)

A small perennial with reddish-green leaves and flowers of almost any hue in spring. The leaves may irritate.

## *Dysoxylum* spp. (red bean, onionwood, pencil cedar)

Rare large evergreen trees with long glossy dark green leaves and small white fragrant bell-shaped flowers. Both the wood and the bark can irritate the skin.

## *Dysphania* spp. (red crumbweed)

A tiny annual with a red stem, pale green leaves and small white flowers. The sap can irritate.

## Eastern red cedar, see *Juniperus virginiana*

## *Ecballium elaterium* (squirting cucumber)

A small climber, either annual or perennial. It has green heart-shaped leaves with yellow bell-shaped leaves. Most of the plant is capable of irritating.

## *Echinopogon* spp. (bearded grass, rough bearded grass, hedgehog grass)

Perennial grasses to 50 centimetres.

## *Echium vulgare* (Paterson's curse)

A perennial to 1 metre, with a hairy erect unbranching stem, bluish-green leaves, and rose-pink flowers, which go blue or purple, appear in spring and summer. Apart from hayfever, skin irritation from Paterson's curse is fairly common.

## Elephant's ear, cunjevoi, see *Alocasia macrorrhiza*

## *Equisetum arvense* (horsetail)

A spiky perennial with flesh-coloured stems. The spines may irritate the skin.

## *Eremophila freelingii* (limestone fuschia)

An evergreen shrub with slender branching stems, grey-green leaves and blue tubular flowers in spring. The leaves and the sap may irritate.

## *Eucalyptus staigeriana* (lemon scented ironbark)

A tall evergreen tree with hard grey bark, pale green leaves and clusters of fluffy white flowers in summer. The sap may irritate.

## Fishtail palm, see *Caryota mitis*

## *Gaillardia* spp. (blanket flower)

An annual or perennial to 60 centimetres with grey-green leaves and daisy-like flowers of different colours in autumn. The sap may irritate.

## *Gelsemium sempervirens* (Carolina jessamine, yellow jessamine, evening trumpet flower)

An evergreen climber with yellow funnel-shaped flowers. The nectar is irritant, and the roots, nectar and flowers are all poisonous.

## *Gingko biloba* (maidenhair tree)

See Chapter 9 for details of this tree, any part of which may irritate the skin.

## Globe artichoke, see *Cynaria scolymus*

## *Hakea* spp.

See Chapter 8 for details of this species, whose leaves may irritate the skin.

## *Helenium* spp. (sneezeweed)

A perennial to 2 metres with yellow daisy-like flowers with brown centres. The seeds and the plant may irritate.

## *Helichrysum blandowskianum* (woolly everlasting daisy)

A perennial with grey hairy leaves and small white papery daisy-like flowers. The hairs are irritant.

## *Heliotropium* spp. (cherry pie, sunray, hoary sunray)

Small shrubs or perennial or annual plants. They have dull green leaves with tubular flowers of yellow or lilac. Any part of the plant, but especially the leaves, may irritate the skin.

# Hemlock, carrot fern, see *Conium maculatum*

## *Heracleum sphondylium* (hogwood)

A biennial plant to 2 metres with a thick rigid hollow stem, 60 centimetre long green leaves and small white-pink flowers in summer. Any part of the plant may be highly irritant.

## *Heteropogon contortus* (black spear grass)

A perennial grass to 1 metre with brownish-grey flowers. The seeds may irritate.

## *Humulus lupulus* (hop)

A perennial climber with a rough prickly stem and yellow-green flowers. The sap is irritant.

## *Hura crepitans* (sandbox tree)

A large evergreen tree with small red flowers. The seeds and sap may irritate.

## *Impatiens non-tangere* (touch-me-not)

A variety of impatiens with large yellow flowers in summer. The sap is highly irritant.

# Incense cedar, see *Libocedrus decurrens*

## *Inula graveolens* (stinkwort)

A small annual plant with yellow flowers, which can irritate.

## *Ipomoea batatas* (sweet potato vine)

A slender perennial climber with heart-shaped leaves and large pinkish-mauve trumpet-shaped flowers. The leaves may be irritant.

## *Isotoma* spp. (rock poison)

A small spreading annual or perennial with bright green leaves. The sap causes skin irritation.

### *Isotropis* spp. (poison sage, lamb poison)

A small perennial with hairy stems, sparse leaves, and yellow, orange or purple pea-shaped flowers. Any part of the plant may be irritating.

### *Jasminium officinale* (poet's jasmine)

A slender evergreen climber with dark green leaves and clusters of fragrant white tubular flowers in summer. The strong perfume may be irritating.

### *Juniperus virginiana* (eastern red cedar)

A tall evergreen tree with reddish-brown bark and small dark berries. The leaves are needle-like on juvenile plants and scale-like on mature plants. The wood may cause irritation.

### Jute, see *Cochorus olitorius*

### Kurrajong, bottle tree, see *Brachychiton* spp.

### *Lactuca serriola* (prickly lettuce, wild lettuce)

A perennial to 1.5 metres with blue-green leaves which may irritate.

### Lady's slipper, see *Cypripedium* spp.

### *Lambertia formosa* (mountain devil)

A large evergreen with dark green leaves and red, tubular flowers, occurring in clusters of seven, in spring and summer. The sap may irritate.

### *Legnephora moorei* (native grape)

An evergreen vine with a weak, twisting stem, heart-shaped leaves and red grapes. The leaves may irritate.

### Lemon-scented ironbark, see *Eucalyptus staigeriana*

### *Leonurus cardiaca*

A perennial to 1 metre with a square stem and pink or white flowers in late summer, which may cause irritation.

## *Libocedrus decurrens* (incense cedar)

A large evergreen tree with tiny scale-like overlapping leaves and cones. The sap may irritate.

## *Ligustrum* (privet)

Evergreen shrubs or trees with dark green leaves, black berries and clusters of small white flowers in summer. The perfume may be irritating, the pollen may cause asthma and hayfever, and the leaves and bark may irritate.

## Limestone fuchsia, see *Eremophila freelingii*

## *Lomatia silaifolia* (crinkle bush)

An evergreen shrub to 1.5 metres. The leaves are deeply serrated and the flowers are creamy and Grevillea-like, appearing in summer. The perfume of the flowers may be irritating.

## *Lotus* spp.

A small perennial which may spread as ground cover. It has greyish leaves and red, yellow or rose-pink flowers, whose perfume may irritate.

## *Maclura pomifera* (Osage orange, bow wood)

A medium-sized deciduous tree with oblong green leaves and greenish-yellow fruit. Various parts may irritate.

## *Mangifera indica* (mango)

A tall tropical evergreen tree with long, dark green leaves and red or yellow flowers. The skin or the juice of the fruit may cause allergic reactions.

## *Medicago sativa* (Medick, burr trefoil, woolly burr)

A perennial plant to 1 metre with bluish-purple pea-like leaves in summer, fruit and spirally coiled pods. Any part of the plant may irritate.

## *Melaleuca leucadendra* (cajuput)

A large evergreen tree with long, pale grey leaves, and bottlebrush-like flowers of creamy-white, pink or green in winter. The fruit are woody capsules. Various parts of the tree may irritate the skin.

## Merium oleander (oleander)

A large evergreen shrub with long, narrow dark green leaves, pink or white flowers, and pods containing hairy seeds. The leaves are poisonous, and any part of the plant may irritate.

## Monstera deliciosa (fruit salad plant)

A robust perennial with strong, crooked stems, aerial roots, glossy green leaves and fruit that look like green sweet corn. Any part of the plant may be highly irritant.

## Moonflower, see *Calonyction aculeatum*

## Morus rubra (red mulberry)

A large spreading deciduous tree with rough leaves and red mulberries. The leaves and bark may be an irritant.

## Mountain devil, see *Lambertia formosa*

## Musa acuminata cultivars (banana tree)

A medium-sized evergreen tree with stout, glossy green trunk, large leaves, yellow flowers and bananas (hopefully). The skins of unripe fruit can irritate.

## Native couch, see *Brachyachne* spp.

## Native grape, see *Legnephora moorei*

## Nicotiana spp. (wild tobacco)

An annual or perennial plant to 1.5 metres, with large dull green and white tubular flowers. Any part of the plant may irritate.

## Oleander see, *Merium oleander*

## Opuntia spp. (prickly pear)

A large evergreen plant with a straight stem, large bright yellow funnel-shaped flowers, and prickly pears as fruit. Touching them is dangerous because of the spikes.

Pasque flower, see *Anemone pulsatilla*

Paterson's curse, see *Echium vulgare*

Paw paw, see *Carica papaya*

Pineapple, see *Ananas comosus*

Poison walnut, see *Cryptocarya pleurosperma*

*Polygonum fagopyrum* (buckwheat)

A medium-sized annual with white flowers. Any part of the plant may irritate.

*Populus deltoides* (cottonwood)

The cottonwood is fairly harmless when dry, but its white seed fibres can irritate when wet.

Prickly pear, see *Opuntia* spp.

Privet, see *Ligustrum* spp.

*Pulsatilla vulgaris* (pasque flower)

A small perennial with a slender stem and a solitary violet flower on top. Any part of the plant may irritate.

Queensland itch tree, see *Davidsonia pruriens*

Quince, see *Cydonia oblonga*

*Rhododendron* spp. (azaleas)

The leaves of azaleas contain toxins which can be an irritant. For details of the plant, see Chapter 8.

Rio rosewood, see *Dalbergia* spp.

Rock poison, see *Isotoma* spp.

Rubber vine, see *Cryptostegia grandiflora*

Scarlet pimpernel, see *Anagallis arvensis*

Shepherd's purse, see *Capsella bursa pastoris*

Sneezeweed, see *Helenium* spp.

Squirting cucumber, see *Ecballium elaterium*

Stinkwort, see *Inula graveolens*

Sundew, see *Drosera* spp.

Sweet potato vine, see *Ipomoea batatas*

Tree of heaven, see *Ailanthus altissima*

Trumpet vine, see *Campsis radicans*

Wallaby grass, see *Danthonia* spp.

Water plantain, see *Alisma plantago aquatica*

Wild ginger, see *Asarum* spp.

Wild tobacco, see *Nicotiana* spp.

Woolly everlasting daisy, see *Helichrysum blandowskianum*

## PERFUMES

Some plants with extremely strong perfumes can irritate. Gardenias, jasmines and lilac can all induce hayfever and asthma.

---

It would be hard to keep in mind all the plants listed in this chapter, but it comes down to something fairly simple. If it's hairy, or spiky, or has milky sap, then don't touch it.

---

# Part IV
# GOOD GARDENING

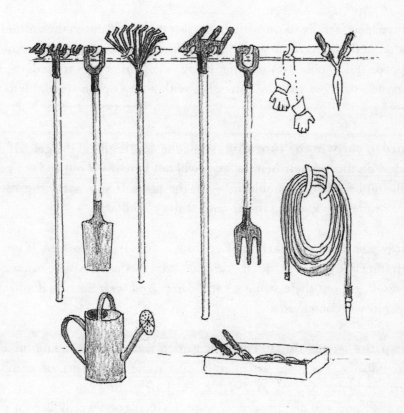

Low Allergy Gardening •

What Else Can You Do? • Where To Get Help

# CHAPTER 17
# LOW ALLERGY GARDENING

There's much more to gardening than just sticking plants in the ground and watering them every now and then. Even if your garden is full of milky-sapped, spiky, pollen-producing living allergens, you can reduce your exposure to those risks by gardening with a few tips in mind. Here they are.

**Garden early in the morning,** while the dew is still on the grass. If there is dew on the ground, then the grass will not have dried out and the pollen will still be where it should be – on the plant. If you want to garden at other times of the day, wait for cool, damp or dull days.

**Mow the lawn regularly**, and get to it before it goes to seed. If you can get somebody else to do it for you, even better. If you're mowing it yourself, get out there while it's still damp. And wear a mask, if you don't feel too self-conscious.

**Keep the weeds down**. For your garden beds, it means using mulch or groundcover. For your lawns, it means using some sort of combined fertiliser/herbicide such as Weed 'n' Feed, or getting out there while the grass is damp and digging the weeds out. Get a good weedkiller for paths, corners and up against the fence.

**Have a clean-out twice a year**. At the start of spring and the end of summer, go through the backyard (and front) and throw out everything you don't need.

**Be vicious with privet.** Have no mercy.

**Drain any damp areas**, as these can allow moulds and algae to grow, many of which are allergenic. Wash garbage cans regularly, for the same reason.

**Avoid gardening on windy days,** as there is much more pollen around on those days. Stay indoors if you can on those days.

**Wear wraparound sunglasses** if you get itchy eyes, as they may reduce the amount of pollen reaching the eyes.

**If you want wind-pollinated plants,** don't put them near your windows, as they are more likely to get inside. Most pollens travel only short distances.

**Avoid strong-smelling plants.**

**Talk to your neighbours about what's in their garden.** If they have privet that's constantly getting into your place, or making you wheezy when you go near it, offer to help remove it.

**Don't hang your washing outside**, especially your bedclothes, on hot windy days during the high pollen season. I know it's the best time to wash them, because they dry quickly, but wait for a stiller day.

**Use airconditioning.** If you have it, use it during hot weather in the pollen season, but make sure you have maintained it and cleaned the filters regularly.

**Create a garden to reduce the effect of pollution** if you feel it contributes to your allergy problems, or makes your asthma worse in any way, and you live near a busy road. A good thick garden at the front will reduce the amount of pollution coming directly into your house. It won't reduce the amount of pollution in your suburb, but it will stop it flowing straight through your open front door. You probably need a layer of shrubs and small trees 5 to 10 metres thick.

**Be creative.** Think about what else can go in your garden. A garden is more than a collection of grass and plants. You can use furniture, pots, statues, water, paints, sheds, seats and screens. Consider the alternatives to azaleas and glossy abelia.

**Use mulch.** This is such a tricky one, that it's worth a whole chapter to itself.

## LOW ALLERGY PEST CONTROL

In general, whatever pest control you want to use is fine, as long as you don't spray it all over yourself or sniff the can. Avoid windy days, and wear a mask, long sleeves and gloves. Pyrethrum-based pesticides are fairly gentle, and not too many people have problems with them. Most of the chemicals we use are toxic, but not necessarily allergenic.

An advantage of using the bird-pollinated plants recommended in chapters 7 to 13 is that if you do that, you will attract more birds to the garden. These will eat some of the garden pests, encouraging healthier plants and reducing the need for sprays. This, in turn, will encourage the return of ladybirds, which are wonderful natural pesticides.

# Mulches

Composting and mulching are controversial among the experts who are interested in developing a low allergy garden.

Basically, the people who are approaching a low allergy garden from the health side believe you should not use organic mulches, whether that be compost or woodchip, as they harbour mould spores. These may worsen asthma and hayfever.

The people who look at a low allergy garden from the gardening side believe that you can't have a garden without compost and mulch. They would argue that the advantages of composting are that you are saving nutrients from the soil and returning them to the soil, that you are covering the soil and preventing weed growth, that you are reducing the need for fertiliser and water, and that you are stopping soil from splashing up onto leaves and causing problems.

I favour the second approach, and think that you can't have a good garden without compost and mulch. While there is no doubt that compost and mulch harbour spores, and that these will worsen allergies when stirred up, using mulch has many advantages for people with allergies.

If you mulch, you will have to dig the garden less often. You will have to weed less often. You will require less fertiliser. You will have to spend less time working in the garden. And there will be fewer weeds giving off pollen.

So if you are aiming for a low maintenance garden, mulching is a necessity. You can use either slow decay mulches or quick decay mulches.

## DON'T DIG

If you are going to use mulch, and are sensitive to moulds, then disturb the mulch as little as possible once it is spread. This will reduce the amount of mould stirred up.

# Slow decay mulches

If you talk to asthma or allergy experts about what mulch you should use in your garden, they will tell you that something inorganic like gravel, pebbles or large rocks are ideal.

While these materials provide few hiding places for spores, and do reduce the allergen load in a garden, they are ugly, boring and return nothing to the soil. They can look good in the right type of garden, such as a formal Japanese-style garden, but frequently look out of place in the more relaxed style of garden most commonly found in Australia and New Zealand.

One place where this style of mulch is suitable is in the very small garden, such as those behind city terrace houses. Here, a fine pebble mulch and paving can make a small garden easy to maintain and, if designed well, seem larger than it is.

The more common slow decay mulches used are pinebark and woodchip. These are organic materials which will decay very slowly, taking between five and twenty years to break down completely.

If used in a thick layer of 10 centimetres or so, these will reduce weed growth significantly so that all you need to do is stoop occasionally to pull out a couple of feeble-looking stragglers that are growing in the mulch, not the soil.

Woodchip and pinebark return little to the soil, but they provide enough air for worms to flourish.

# Quick decay mulches

These are basically composts. You get your grass clippings, your fallen leaves, your vegetable scraps and anything else organic you have lying around, and throw them in a pile. Add a little water (if it's dry), maybe a little soil, a few worms if you have them, and let the pile cook for three to six months. Then spread around the garden, nice and thick. At least 10 centimetres is needed to keep the weeds down.

This is a very simple-minded approach, and might offend the people who devote their lives to composting. But it's a start in the right direction.

The advantages of using compost as mulch is that it returns nutrients to the soil, it encourages good plant growth and it reduces the amount of garden and household refuse you have to put in the bin or take to the tip. With the rapid increase in tip fees of the past few years, it is a real money-saving exercise.

Composting works best if you have two or three separate piles going at once. You get the first one up, then get the second one, then pile up the third. Then you spread the first pile around, and replace it with your clippings, leaves and other material.

A word of warning. Few plants like to have mulch right up to their stems or trunks. Most like a little breathing space. Citrus, Rhododendrons, Camellias and Magnolias are all highly susceptible to disease from close mulching. So, when spreading mulch, it's wise to leave a little breathing space around the stem or trunk.

## LOW ALLERGY COMPOSTING

If you want to compost, and you have allergies, there are a number of ways you can reduce your exposure to the spores, moulds and pollens that may have gathered.

**Use a closed compost system** such as a bin, as this reduces the amount of allergen floating through the air.

**Ask somebody else to spread the compost** when it needs to be spread as mulch.

**Wet the mulch slightly** when you are working in the garden and disturbing the mulch. This will reduce the amount of floating allergen (although not too much, as you shouldn't work with wet soil).

**Wear a light mask,** as when you are using using sprays and pesticides.

# CHAPTER 18
# WHAT ELSE CAN YOU DO?

There are many other things you can do to help reduce the toll of allergy. What you decide to do really depends on what triggers your allergies. The list of possibilities is long and includes the following suggestions.

- Ensure you take prescribed medication regularly.
- Avoid foods to which you are allergic.
- Consider having allergy injections/desensitisation.
- Avoid irritants for angry skin.
- Monitor your asthma.
- Avoid pets.
- Keep windows closed during times of high pollen or wind.
- Avoid emotional stress.
- Avoid aspirin if it bothers you.
- Avoid irritants.
- Consider whether or not your work is playing a part.
- Avoid catching a cold.
- Prepare for exercise.
- Watch out for thunderstorms.
- Reduce the number of dust mites in your house.
- Get rid of mould.

We'll go through each of these suggestions one at a time.

# Ensure you take prescribed medication regularly

It is quite easy to remember to take medication when you are feeling sick. You have a pill or a potion or a puffer that you know will make you feel better, and you feel bad, so you can see the connection. Sick, pill, better. It's almost Pavlovian.

But it's quite hard to remember to take medications when you feel well, or at least fairly well. Most people with asthma find it a struggle to remember to take their preventive puffers like Intal or Pulmicort or Becotide every day, whether they are feeling wheezy or not. They find it hard to take something which reminds them they have a chronic illness, especially when they are trying their hardest to forget that they have one. The thing to remember is this: preventive medications work. If you take them, your next bout of asthma may last a week or two, and you won't end up in hospital. If you stop taking them as soon as you feel better, your next bout of asthma may last three months, including a few nights in the local hospital. Preventive medications may not prevent you getting asthma, but they certainly do prevent it getting on top of you.

# Avoid foods to which you are allergic

A small proportion of people with asthma, hayfever and urticaria are allergic to certain foods. Nuts are a common stimulus to allergy, and quite a few people say they swell up when they eat chocolate (although that's probably fat, not allergy). The other more common causes of food allergy are shellfish, milk, eggs and some seeds. That type of allergy is fairly easy to deal with – avoid the foods that you know cause problems.

But there is a hidden problem affecting a small number of people with asthma – perhaps 10 per cent or so. That is a reaction to metabisulphite.

Metabisulphite is a preservative which is used mainly to stop bacteria from growing in foods and drinks. It also stops food browning, and stops vitamin C from leaching out of fruit juices. Under Australia's national food labelling scheme, metabisulphite is additive number 220, 223 and 224.

Following is a list of foods and drinks which are likely to contain metabisulphite. Think about it and see – is your asthma worse after consuming something from this list?

| DRINKS | FRUIT | VEGETABLES | MEAT AND SEAFOOD |
|---|---|---|---|
| wine, especially sweet white wine | dried tree fruits – apples, apricots, pears, peaches and mixed dried fruit with peel (sultanas, currants, raisins and prunes have no metabisulphite) | pickles | sausages and sausage mince |
| champagne | | pickled onions, gherkins etc | frankfurts |
| alcoholic cider | | instant mashed potatoes | luncheon meats such as devon and pressed chicken |
| some beers | | pre-peeled and pre-cut potatoes | |
| some coloured soft drinks | | potato crisps (some) | salamis, bratwursts and other processed meats |
| bottled drinks containing fruit juice | ready-made fresh fruit salad from a shop (metabisulphite may be added illegally to stop fruit browning) | | green prawns |
| some chilled fruit juices | | | |
| cordial | | | |

## THE PICKLED ONION TEST

You should only do this test if you have your reliever medication on hand.

One way of finding out whether you are sensitive to these preservatives is the pickled onion test. Get a pickled onion. Eat it. Get another one and eat it, too.

Are you wheezy? Do you have any tightness in your chest? If so, then you are probably allergic to preservatives number 220, 223 and 224.

A small number of people with asthma are also sensitive to MSG, or monosodium glutamate. While MSG is best known as an additive used in many Chinese restaurants, it is found naturally in tomatoes, mushrooms and some cheeses, such as Parmesan, Camembert and blue vein.

MSG can also be found in large quantities in prepared products such as soy sauce, oyster sauce, pizza and takeaway chicken. It may also be found in smaller quantities in foods such as:
• packet and canned soups;
• Italian foods;
• pies and sausage rolls;
• frankfurts;
• canned and delicatessen luncheon meats;
• meat and fish pastes;
• frozen prepared dishes;
• canned vegetables in sauces;
• flavoured potato crisps;
• mixed and spiced seasonings;
• gravy makers;
• stock cubes;
• tomato juice, paste and sauce;
• seasoned bread crumbs;
• stuffing mixes;
• meat tenderisers.

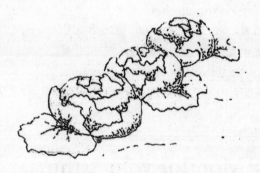

*Brassica oleracea (cabbage)*

# Consider having allergy injections/desensitisation

Occasionally, very severe spring hayfever symptoms do not respond to any kind of oral antihistamines or nasal sprays and may benefit from pollen desensitising injections. Pollen sensitive asthma, which is well controlled at other times of the year, but unstable in the spring, and requiring great increases of preventer medication or oral steroids may also gain benefit from pollen desensitising injections.

In the case of pollen sensitive asthma, desensitising injections should only be initiated by a specialist allergist and the treatment carried out by a general practitioner under the supervision of a specialist allergist.

The benefits and side effects should be carefully explained by the specialist before treatment is commenced. The injection program is started after the pollen season is over and when the asthma is stable. Severe, life threatening reactions have occurred when strict guidelines have not been followed.

# Avoid irritants for angry skin

If you have eczema or contact dermatitis, there are many ways to reduce the damage to your skin and the itch that's driving you mad.
• Avoid known allergens and irritants such as coarse woollen or synthetic clothes.
• Wear loose-fitting cotton clothes.
• Take short cool showers, rather than long hot showers, to prevent the skin drying out.
• Use lotions or soap substitutes instead of soap.
• Use an appropriate moisturiser such as sorbolene at least three times daily.
• Try not to scratch.

# Monitor your asthma

The best way to monitor your asthma is through an objective measure such as the peak flow meter. This is a cylinder about 25 centimetres long, with a measuring scale up one side. You blow into the end as hard as possible, and it gives a reading of the force of air expired.

If you measure your peak flow rate with this meter each morning and evening before taking any medication, then take another reading 10 minutes after medication, you will soon find out what your best readings are, and you will soon notice dips below those best readings. Sometimes, your peak flow reading will dip below your best before you even feel any asthma. You will also discover your response to medication.

You can discuss this with your doctor, and work out a plan of action based on your peak flow readings. The aim of this plan is to reduce the severity of any asthma attack you may get.

A typical asthma management plan is reproduced on the following pages. Your doctor would simply fill in the gaps, then you stick it on your fridge and act on it.

In Australia, copies of this plan can be obtained from the National Asthma Campaign on 1800 032 495.

## CHILDREN

Children under the age of five or six cannot usually use a peak flow meter properly. Their asthma can be assessed using a symptom score card, also available from the Asthma Foundation.

# ASTHMA ACTION PLAN

Name _____ Date _____ Best Peak Flow _____

(6 years and over)

| WHEN WELL | PEAK FLOW |
|---|---|
| Take preventer (if prescribed) | Above: |
| Name _____ Name _____ | |
| Dose _____ Dose _____ | |
| How often _____ How often _____ | _____ |
| Take reliever _____ Dose _____ | |
| (Take only when necessary for relief of symptoms) | |
| Before exercise, take:_____ | |

| WHEN NOT WELL | PEAK FLOW |
|---|---|
| At the first sign of a cold or if asthma symptoms get worse: | Between: |
| Take reliever _____ | |
| Dose _____ How often _____ | _____ |
| Take preventer (if prescribed) _____ | |
| Name_____ Name _____ | and |
| Dose _____ Dose _____ | |
| How often _____ How often _____ | _____ |
| *When your symptoms get better, return to the When Well doses* | |

| IF SYMPTOMS GET WORSE | PEAK FLOW |
|---|---|
| Extra steps to take: | Less than: |
| ☐ _____ | |
| ☐ _____ | |
| ☐ _____ | _____ |
| ☐ Emergency Medication _____ Dose _____ | |
| Take _____ | |
| _____ | |
| _____ | |

## IF YOU FOLLOW THIS PLAN BUT YOUR SYMPTOMS GET WORSE, SEE A DOCTOR IMMEDIATELY OR CALL AN AMBULANCE

Ambulance: _____ Doctor Tel: _____ Hospital: _____

_____ Tel (AH): _____

# ASTHMA ACTION PLAN

| WHEN WELL | PEAK FLOW |
|---|---|
| You will <br><br> ☐ be free of regular night-time wheeze or cough or chest tightness <br> ☐ have no regular wheeze or cough or chest tightness on waking or during the day <br> ☐ be able to take part in normal physical activity without getting asthma symptoms <br> ☐ need reliever medication less than 3–4 times a week (except if it is used before exercise). | At or about personal best readings |

| WHEN NOT WELL | PEAK FLOW |
|---|---|
| You will <br><br> ☐ have increasing night-time wheeze or cough or chest tightness <br> ☐ have symptoms regularly in the morning when you wake-up <br> ☐ have a need for extra doses of reliever medication <br> ☐ have symptoms which interfere with exercise <br><br><br><br> (You may experience one or more of these) | Increasing difference between morning and evening readings (before reliever) <br><br> Readings generally 60–80% of best |

| IF SYMPTOMS GET WORSE, THIS IS AN ACUTE ATTACK | PEAK FLOW |
|---|---|
| You will <br><br> ☐ have one or more of the following: wheeze, cough, chest tightness or shortness of breath <br> ☐ need to use your reliever medication at least once every 3 hours or more often | Generally less than 50–60% of personal best |
| DANGER SIGNS <br><br> ☐ your symptoms get worse very quickly <br> ☐ wheeze or chest tightness or shortness of breath continue after using reliever medication or return within minutes of taking reliever medication <br> ☐ severe shortness of breath, inability to speak comfortably, blueness of lips | Less than 30% of usual best |
| IMMEDIATE ACTION IS NEEDED—CALL AN AMBULANCE | |

*Take this action plan with you when you visit your doctor.*

Reproduced courtesy of the National Asthma Campaign,
the Australasian Paediatric Respiratory Group and Rhône-Poulenc Australia Pty Ltd

# Avoid pets

Animals and birds have scales on their skin known as dander. These shed, causing major problems for some people with allergies.

In Australia and New Zealand, cats are by far the worst culprits, as they shed hair and dander all over the place. But all pets have the potential to cause allergies, and there is no such thing as a non-allergenic animal.

Some people believe that short-haired cats are going to cause fewer problems than long-haired cats, or that small short-haired dogs will be OK. They will be, if you are not allergic to dander. But if you are, then any animal – bird, guinea pig, dog, cat or pet rat – can cause you problems.

If you have a pet that lives inside, get it outside and keep it there. Then wait – it can take three to six months for all the hair and dander throughout your house to settle down. Never let it back in the house. Some people find it necessary to get rid of pets completely.

If you wonder whether your pet could be causing you problems, think about what happened when you went away on holidays and left the pet behind. Did your asthma or hayfever clear up? If so, your pet could well be playing a part in your illness.

# Keep windows closed during times of high pollen or wind

If it's windy, or if there is plenty of pollen around (some cities give daily pollen counts), then keeping your windows closed will reduce the amount of pollen that gets into your house.

# Avoid emotional stress

This can be incredibly difficult to do, considering that emotional stress usually occurs because a situation is difficult to control. But emotional stress can make some allergy-based problems, particularly eczema, worse.

# Avoid aspirin if it bothers you

A small proportion of asthmatics are sensitive to aspirin and other anti-inflammatory drugs, and become wheezy if they walk past the aspirin packets in the supermarket. If this is you, avoid them.

# Avoid irritants

If you have asthma, you shouldn't smoke, and you shouldn't allow anyone to smoke in the house where you live. Some people find it difficult to go to pubs, clubs and other places where the pall of cigarette smoke hangs low.

Air pollution, overall, is not a cause of asthma. But some people are sensitive to it, and find their asthma worsens on high pollution days. If this is the case with you, you should stay inside when pollution is high.

Some people also find that the fumes from paints, household cleaners and perfumes exacerbate their asthma.

# Consider whether or not your work is playing a part

Some work environments can be harmful to people with asthma, and some workplaces can induce asthma in people who have never had it before. The most common dangers at work seem to be wood dusts, flour and industrial chemicals such as resins and metal salts. It is possible that volatile organic chemicals and formaldehyde also play a part.

# Avoid catching a cold

Many people with asthma find that an attack is induced by a cold or the flu. While it is very hard to avoid catching a cold, you could try to do so by:

- keeping warm and dry whenever possible;
- avoiding people with colds and making sure that they don't sneeze near you;
- taking 500 milligrams of vitamin C each day; and
- in winter, wearing warm clothes and keeping windows open.

Nobody has shown scientifically that vitamin C helps prevent a cold. Then again, nobody has shown scientifically that getting cold and wet will allow a cold to develop, but we accept that as true. The vitamin C, even if it doesn't help, won't hurt.

# Prepare for exercise

When you're standing around, dreaming of winning Lotto or of a life without cats, you breathe somewhere between 5 and 10 litres of air each minute. When you start running around, you may be breathing anywhere up to 100 litres of air each minute.

As all this air comes in, your upper airways warm it and moisten it in preparation for its descent into your lungs. Unfortunately, the loss of warmth and moisture from your airways into the air may induce asthma.

If you are one of those people who get asthma when they exercise, you can prepare for it. Warm up exercises may prevent asthma in some people. Two puffs of Intal, Tilade or Vicrom taken five minutes before exercise is very good at preventing exercise-induced asthma , and two puffs of reliever medication can work almost as well. If your exercise-induced asthma is severe, take both.

Another way of preparing for exercise is to warm up gently for 20 minutes before the strenuous exercise begins. This works almost as well as the puffers.

If you don't have any warning, a couple of quick puffs of Intal, Tilade or a reliever even during the exercise can help. It also helps to breathe through your nose, as that warms and humidifies the air before it reaches your lungs.

# Watch out for thunderstorms

Over the past decade, doctors started noticing that hospitals were overwhelmed with asthmatics during and after thunderstorms.

One of the most striking epidemics of asthma in Australia came during a thunderstorm which hit Wagga Wagga, in south-western New South Wales, at about 8pm on 13 November 1993. Springtime.

Immediately, the emergency department of Wagga Wagga Hospital was flooded with asthmatics. Usually, fewer than ten asthmatics a day go to the hospital, but eighty appeared for treatment during and after that storm.

Interviews conducted afterwards revealed that most of them had started to feel wheezy in the three hours before the storm hit, and that 20 per cent had never had asthma before, although some had suffered from hayfever.

Why should thunderstorms cause asthma? It seems the rain and the highly electrically charged atmosphere encourages the rye-grass grains to split, allowing the release of hundreds of highly allergenic starch particles.

These are blown along by strong winds and breathed into the lungs of susceptible people, where they do their stuff.

Keeping inside during thunderstorms should reduce the chances of an asthma attack occurring.

# Reduce the number of dust mites in your house

Dust mites are tiny insects, too small to be visible without a microscope. They have been recognised in the past decade as one of the major triggers of asthma, hayfever and other allergies. It is actually not the mite that is the problem, nor the dust so much, but the mite's faeces. They are highly allergenic.

House dust mites thrive in warm, dark and moist conditions where there is plenty of their favourite food – dried out scales of human skin. So they like bedding, carpets, sofas and comfy chairs and cushions, clothing and soft toys. In fact, they love anything where dust can collect, because that is where our dried out skin goes to die.

There is plenty you can do to keep the amount of dust mite down in your house, and how far you go depends on how bad the problem is, and how zealous you are. The list includes the following.

• Rip up the carpets and replace them with something that can be mopped, whether that be polished boards, vinyl, cork, slate or parquetry.
• Put plastic covers on your mattresses and pillows.
• Keep soft toys out of beds.
• Wash bedding in hot water and dry it in the sun for four hours – although avoid windy days as the bedding will pick up other allergens.
• Replace venetian blinds and heavy drapes with holland or vertical blinds.
• Keep the house tidy, and don't allow piles of rubbish to build up.
• Don't store anything on top of wardrobes or under beds.
• Use a damp cloth for dusting, not a feather duster.

# Get rid of mould

Moulds can be potent allergens. They are found most often in bathrooms, kitchens and walk-in wardrobes. Sometimes you can see moulds, or sometimes you just pick up a musty smell.

If you want to get rid of mould, you have to deal with whatever has allowed it in the house. Mouldy walls may require a new dampcourse in the house, while mouldy bathrooms may need an extraction fan, leaks from the shower plugged or roof tiles fixed.

Indoor pot plants have mould in the soil.

---

**A BELL**

If somebody in your family has severe asthma, it would be wise to keep a bell by their bed. That way if they wake and need help urgently, they can ring the bell rather than trying to call for help.

---

# WHERE TO
# GET HELP

For Information on Asthma • For Information

on Allergies • For Information on Plants •

For Information on Food Allergies

# AUSTRALIA

## For information on asthma

**Asthma Foundation of New South Wales**
Unit 1, 'Garden Mews'
82–86 Pacific Highway
St Leonards, NSW 2065
Telephone: (02) 9906 3233
Fax: (02) 9906 4493

There are over thirty branches and support groups of the Asthma Foundation across New South Wales. Please telephone the New South Wales office for the name and contact number of your nearest support group.

**Asthma Foundation of the Northern Territory**
PO Box 40456
Casuarina, NT 0811
Telephone: (08) 8922 8817
Fax: (08) 8922 8616

**Asthma Foundation of Queensland**
PO Box 394
Fortitude Valley
Brisbane, Queensland 4006
Telephone: (07) 3252 7677
Fax: (07) 3257 1080

**Asthma Foundation of South Australia**
329 Payneham Road
Royston Park, SA 6070
Telephone: (08) 8362 6272
Fax: (08) 8362 2818

### Asthma Foundation of Tasmania

82 Hampden Road
Battery Point, Tasmania 7000
Telephone: (002) 23 7765
from October 1996 (03) 6223 7765
Fax: (002) 24 2509
from October 1996 (03) 6224 2509

### Asthma Foundation of Victoria

101 Princess Street
Kew, Victoria 3101
Telephone: (03) 9853 5666
Fax: (03) 9853 9196

### Asthma Foundation of Western Australia

2/61 Heytesbury Road
Subiaco, WA 6008
Telephone: (09) 382 1666
from 1997 (08) 9382 1666
Fax: (09) 388 1469
from 1997 (08) 9388 1465

### National Asthma Campaign

615 St Kilda Rd
Melbourne, Victoria 3004
Telephone: (1800) 032 495 or (03) 9214 1414
Fax: (03) 9214 1400
The National Asthma Campaign can also be reached on the Internet.
Its site is http://hna.ffh.vic.gov.au/asthma

## For information on allergies

### Australian Society of Clinical Immunologists and Allergists

PO Box 204
Mount Albert, Victoria 3127

**Hayfever and Allergy Information Service**
Po Box 946
North Sydney, NSW 2060

# For information on plants

**The Society for Growing Australian Plants**
Telephone: (02) 9621 3437

# For information on food allergies

**Department of Health Services**
GPO Box 191B
Hobart, Tasmania 7001
Telephone: (002) 33 3762
from October 1996 (03) 6233 3762

**Health Department of Victoria**
GPO Box 4003
Melbourne, Victoria 3001
Telephone: (03) 9616 7212

**Health Department of Western Australia**
PO Box 8172
Stirling St
Perth, WA 6849
Telephone: (09) 222 4222

**Institute of Public Health**
PO Box 380
North Ryde, NSW 2113
Telephone: (02) 9887 5617

**Northern Territory Department of Health and Community Services**
PO Box 40596
Casuarina, NT 0811
Telephone: (08) 9889 2714

**Public and Environmental Health Service**
Frewin Place
Scullin, ACT 2614
Telephone: (06) 205 1700
(02) 6205 1700

**South Australian Health Commission**
PO Box 6
Rundle Mall
Adelaide, SA 5000
Telephone: (08) 8225 6530

**National Food Authority**
PO Box 7186
Canberra MC, ACT 2610
Telephone: (02) 6271 2222
Fax: (02) 6271 2209

# NEW ZEALAND

## For information on asthma

**Asthma and Respiratory Foundation of New Zealand**
Rossmore House
123 Molesworth Street
Wellington
Telephone: (04) 499 4592
Fax: (04) 499 4594

**Allergy and Hyperactivity – Attention Deficit Disorder Association**
93 Waipapa Road
Hataiti
Wellington
Telephone: (04) 386 2514

**Allergy Awareness Association Inc.**
PO Box 12-701
Auckland 6

**Attention Disorder and Hyperactivity Association**
PO Box 51675
Auckland

**Christchurch Allergy Awareness Association**
PO Box 15-052
Christchurch, 2

**New Zealand Eczema Support Group Inc.**
PO Box 12389
Chartwell Square
Hamilton

# Local asthma societies and branches

| | |
|---|---|
| Ashburton | PO Box 552, Ashburton (03) 308 9556 |
| Auckland | PO Box 67066, Mt Eden, Auckland (09) 630 2293 |
| Buller | 18 Eastons Rd, Westport (03) 789 8349 |
| Canterbury | PO Box 13091, Christchurch (03) 366 5235 |
| Eastern BOP | PO Box 655, Whakatane (07) 308 8467 |
| Gisborne/E. Coast | PO Box 797, Gisborne (06) 868 5041 |
| Gore | 97 Frank St, Gore (03) 208 5293 |
| Hawke's Bay | PO Box 4043, Marewa, Napier (06) 835 0018 |
| Horowhenua | PO Box 60, Levin (06) 368 1114 |
| Kapiti | PO Box 69, Paraparaumu (04) 297 1353 |
| Manawatu | PO Box 5164, Palmerston North (06) 354 7030 |
| Marlborough | PO Box 374, Blenheim (03) 574 2761 |
| Matamata | PO Box 8, Matamata (07) 888 6233 |
| Nelson | PO Box 450, Nelson (03) 544 8557 |
| North Otago | PO Box 16, Oamaru (03) 434 6208 |
| Northland | PO Box 1109, Whangarei (09) 438 5205 |
| Otago | PO Box 5494, Dunedin (03) 477 4983 |
| Rotorua | PO Box 472, Rotorua (07) 347 1012 |

South Canterbury    PO Box 267, Timaru (03) 688 3739

Southland    c/o Ward Wilson, PB 90106, Invercargill
(03) 214 4988

Taranaki    PO Box 186, New Plymouth (06) 758 9195

Tauranga    PO Box 217, Tauranga (07) 577 6738

Waikato    PO Box 15103, Dinsdale, Hamilton (07) 839 4567

Waimate    155 High St, Waimate (03) 689 8524

Wairarapa    PO Box 599, Masterton (06) 377 1175

Wanganui    PO Box 790, Wanganui (06) 343 2855

Wellington    Community Services Centre,
4th Floor Pember House
Hagley Street, Porirua
(04) 237 4520

West Coast    PO Box 428, Greymouth 7801

# Further Reading about Childhood Asthma

The following books are available from asthma societies and book shops or they can be ordered from The Asthma Foundation of New South Wales.

### Childhood Asthma
### What It Is and What You Can Do
DR NEIL BUCHANAN AND DR PETER COOPER
An easily read and delightfully illustrated book for everyone who would like to know more about the problems of asthma in childhood.
Revised edition for Australia and New Zealand
Published by Doubleday

### Your Child with Asthma
DR SIMON GODFREY
A useful and practical book for parents and teachers of children with asthma.
Published by The Asthma Foundation of New South Wales

### All About Asthma
MARIA PRENDERGAST
An informative and useful reference for parents, teachers and health professionals.
Published by Penguin Books, Australia

### Joshua
### Infant & Pre-school Asthma
A handbook for parents and carers of infants and pre-school children with asthma.
It includes practical advice about recognising asthma, modern management strategies, devices and medications, plus a helpful question and answer section.
Published by The Asthma Foundation of Western Australia

### The Chesty Child
DR PETER VAN ASPEREN AND DR CRAIG MELLIS
*The Chesty Child* looks at asthma from infancy to adolescence and answers the questions parents ask when their child is diagnosed with asthma. This comprehensive book is a useful guide for parents, teachers and health professionals.
Published by Ashwood House Medical

## Books for children

### The Asthma Story
DEVELOPED BY 'THE WHEEZERS'
A complete program that teaches children about the nature and effects of asthma and its management. This program is based on the premise that children learn best if they are active in the process. The complete kit includes a large format picture book for 4- to 8-year-olds plus a resource book for presenters or parents. An audio cassette is also available.
Published by 'The Wheezers'

# Further Reading about Plants and Gardening

A wide range of excellent gardening books is available in your local book shop or library if you want more detailed information on the plants you are interested in. You may already have your favourite plant references. The following books are readily available, lavishly illustrated and, referred to in conjunction with Mark Ragg's *The Low Allergy Garden*, will help you choose the right plants to create a garden you can enjoy without sneezing, wheezing, itching, watery eyes or runny noses.

## The Reader's Digest Gardeners' Encyclopedia of Plants and Flowers
The definitive reference work for Australia and New Zealand
Includes over 8000 plants and 4000 photographs
This authoritative reference work provides a comprehensive guide to thousands of plants that can be cultivated in temperate and tropical climates. The main colour section of the book is organised by plant type, size, season of interest and colour which makes it very easy for any gardener to find a specific plant.
Published by Reader's Digest

## Better Homes and Gardens Growers Guide series
This bright, colourful and inexpensive series looks in detail at how to grow popular plants. The easy-to-use format features one plant to a page.
Fully illustrated throughout.
*A Grower's Guide to Annuals*
*A Grower's Guide to Flowering Shrubs*
*A Grower's Guide to Herbs*
*A Growers Guide to Vegetables*
Published by Murdoch Books

## Bay Gardening Library
A comprehensive and reasonably priced series written for the home gardener and lavishly illustrated in colour throughout.
*Annuals & Perennials for Your Garden*
*Bulbs for Your Garden*
*The Food Garden*
*Herbs for Your Garden*
*Planning and Planting Home Gardens*
*Trees and Shrubs for Your Garden*
*Tropical & Warm Climate Gardening*
*The Gardener's Year*
Published by Murdoch Books

# Asthma and Allergy Medication Glossary

**Aldecin** cortiscosteroid spray inhaled to prevent asthma attacks or make the attacks less severe when they do occur. Used daily, Aldecin will also reduce the impact of allergies that trigger hayfever.

**Asmol** relieving medication or bronchodilator for asthma. A version of the drug salbutamol.

**Becloforte** cortiscosteroid medication inhaled to prevent asthma attacks or make the attacks less severe when they do occur.

**Beconase** a preventive nasal spray which will reduce the impact of allergies that trigger hayfever if used daily.

**Becotide** cortiscosteroid medication inhaled to prevent asthma attacks or make the attacks less severe when they do occur.

**Bricanyl** relieving medication or bronchodilator for asthma. A version of the drug terbutaline.

**bronchodilator** a relieving medication inhaled to relax the muscles around the airways, thus allowing you to breathe more easily. Sold as Ventolin, Respolin, Respax, Asmol or Bricanyl.

**Claratyne** a non-sedating antihistamine tablet that will help stop the runny nose and sneezing associated with hayfever.

**corticosteroid** steroid medications that prevent asthma attacks or make attacks less severe if they do occur. Cortiscosteroids can be either inhaled (as Becotide, Becloforte, Aldecin, Pulmicort, Respocort and Flixotide) or taken as tablets (as prednisone). If inhaled at the recommended doses, these steroids are unlikely to produce side effects on the rest of the body. Their effects are restricted to the lungs.

**decongestant sprays** short-term medications for treating hayfever and easing a blocked nose. May damage the lining of the nose if used for prolonged periods.

**Flixotide** cortiscosteroid medication inhaled to prevent asthma attacks or make the attacks less severe when they do occur.

**Hismanal** a non-sedating antihistamine tablet that will help stop the runny nose and sneezing associated with hayfever.

**Indocid** anti-inflammatory medication which can trigger an asthma attack.

**Intal** medication used to prevent asthma attacks or make attacks less severe when they do occur.

**Naprosyn** anti-inflammatory medication which can trigger an asthma attack.

**nebuliser** a pump with a hose and mask attachment. The liquid medication is placed in a bowl attached to the mask. When the nebuliser is switched on, the medication is turned to a fine mist which you breathe in.

**Orudis** anti-inflammatory medication which can trigger an asthma attack.

**peak flow metre** a device which helps you monitor your asthma by providing an objective measure of how bad it is.

**prednisone** cortiscosteroid medication taken in tablet form to prevent asthma attacks or make the attacks less severe when they do occur.

**preventive spray** medications for preventing asthma attacks. These medications dampen down the immune system in the lining of the lungs, so that the lungs don't respond to what usually makes them react. They must be taken every day or they don't work. Brands include Intal, Tilade, Vicrom (in New Zealand) and the corticosteroids Becotide, Becloforte, Aldecin, Pulmicort, Respocort, and Flixotide which can be inhaled and prednosine taken in tablet form.

**puffer** a device used to deliver asthma medication directly to the lungs.

**Pulmicort** cortiscosteroid medication inhaled to prevent asthma attacks, or make the attacks less severe when they do occur.

**RAST test** (Radio-Allergo-Sorbent-Test) a blood test that measures the amount of specific antibodies in your blood.

**relieving medications** bronchodilators for asthma sold as Ventolin, Respolin, Respax or Asmol – versions of salbutamol; or Bricanyl – a version of the drug terbutaline. Relieving medications work by relaxing the muscles around the airways allowing you to breathe more easily. They are very good short-term treatments for asthma.

**Respax** relieving medication or bronchodilator for asthma. A version of the drug salbutamol.

**Respocort** cortiscosteroid medication inhaled to prevent asthma attacks or make the attacks less severe when they do occur

**Respolin** relieving medication or bronchodilator for asthma. A version of the drug salbutamol.

**Rhinalar** a preventive nasal spray which will reduce the impact of allergies that trigger hayfever if used daily.

**Rhinocort** a preventive nasal spray which will reduce the impact of allergies that trigger hayfever if used daily.

**Rynacrom** a preventive nasal spray which will reduce the impact of allergies that trigger hayfever if used daily.

**salbutamol** a drug which is a relieving medication or bronchodilator for asthma. Sold as Ventolin, Respolin, Respax or Asmol. Works by relaxing the muscles around the airways and allowing you to breathe more easily. Very good short-term treatments for asthma attacks.

**skin prick tests** tests for allergies whereby drops containing different allergen extracts are placed on your forearm. The skin is pricked through each allergen extract. After 15 minutes the doctor measures the size and reaction to the different allergen extracts.

**spacer** a device which allows more of a puffer's dose to be delivered to the lungs than a puffer and eliminates the problem of trying to coordinate the puff with the breath. Spacers have a hole in one end, into which the puffer fits. They have a mouthpiece and valve on the other end. You puff the medication into the spacer then slowly breathe it in through the valve.

**steroids** see **cortiscosteroids**.

**Teldane** a non-sedating antihistamine tablet that will help stop the runny nose and sneezing associated with hayfever.

**terbutaline** a relieving medication or bronchodilator for asthma. Sold as Bricanyl.

**Tilade** medication commonly used to prevent asthma attacks or make attacks less severe when they do occur.

**Ventolin** relieving medication or bronchodilator for asthma. A version of the drug salbutamol.

**Vicrom** medication commonly used in New Zealand to prevent asthma attacks or make attacks less severe when they do occur.

**Zyrtec** a non-sedating antihistamine tablet that will help stop the runny nose and sneezing associated with hayfever.

# INDEX

bog onion (*Arisaema*), 106
borage (*Borago officinalis*), 107
boronia, red (*Boronia heterophylla*), 60
bottle tree (*Brachychiton*), 107
bottlebrush (*Callistemon*), 60, 71
bow wood (*Maclura pomifera*), 118
bracelet honey myrtle (*Melaleuca armillaris*),
    63
Brazilian glory pea (*Daubentonia*), 112
breathing, 6–8
    mouth, 16
broad-leaved paperbark (*Melaleuca
    quinquenervia*), 70
bronchodilators, 12
browallia, orange (*Streptosolen jamesonii*), 64
brush wattle (*Albizia lophantha*), 94
bryony, white (*Bryonia*), 107
buckwheat (*Polygonum fagopyrum*), 120
buffalo grass (*Stenotaphrum secundatum*), 72,
    74
bugloss (Borago officinalis), 107
bulbs, 52
burdock (*Arctium lappa*), 105
burr trefoil (*Medicago sativa*), 118
burweeds, yellow (*Amsinchia*), 104
busy Lizzie (*Impatiens wallerana*), 54
button grass (*Dactyloctenium radulans*), 112

C

cabbage tree palm (*Livistona australis*), 70
cajuput (*Melaleuca leucadendra*), 118
calendula (*Calendula officinalis*), 100
Californian lilac (*Ceanothus cyaneus*), 61
camellia, 60–61
canary grass (*Phalaris aquatica*), 76
Canary Island pine (*Pinus canariensis*), 71
canary sassafras (*Doryphora sassafras*), 113
Canterbury bells (*Campanula*), 78
capsicum, 108
Carolina jessamine (*Gelsemium sempervirens*),
    115
carrot fern (*Conium maculatum*), 111
cars, 23
cashew nut (*Anarcardium occidentalis*), 104
cats, 138
cayenne (*Capsicum*), 108
cedar, eastern red (*Juniperus virginiana*), 117
cedar, incense (*Libocedrus decurrens*), 118
cedar, pencil (*Dysoxylum*), 114

cedar, white (*Melia azedarach*), 96
celandine poppy (*Chelidonium majus*), 110
century plant (*Agave*), 103
chamomile (*Anthemis*), 98, 105
cherry, flowering (*Prunus serrulata*), 71
cherry pie (*Heliotropium*), 115
chest tightness, 8
children and asthma, 135
Chilean jasmine (*Mandevilla laxa*), 83
chili pepper (*Capsicum*), 108
Chinese gooseberry (*Actinidia deliciosa*), 82
chives (*Allium schoenoprasum*), 87, 104
cinnamon (*Cinnamomum zeylandicum*), 110
citrus trees, 68
clarkia, 53
cleaners, 139
clematis, 82–83, 110
climbers, 81–85
coal dust, 23
coast banksia (*Banksia integrifolia*), 67
coastal rosemary (*Westringia fruticosa*), 65
cocksfoot (*Dactylis glomerata*), 76
coffee senna (*Cassia*), 109
coffee tree (*Coffea arabica*), 111
cohosh, blue (*Caulophyllum thalictroides*), 109
colds, 139
coleus (*Solenostemon scutellarioides*), 56
columbine (*Aquilegia*), 52
composting, 128–129
contact dermatitis, 19, 100–101
coprosma, 94
coral pea, dusky (*Kennedia rubicunda*), 83
cornflower (*Centaurea cyanus*), 53
correa, white (*Correa alba*), 61
corticosteroids, 10
cotoneaster (*Cotoneaster conspicuus 'Decorus'*),
    61
cottonwood (*Populus deltoides*), 97, 120
cotula filicula, 78
couch, native (*Brachyachne*), 107
couch 'Greenlees Park'(*Cynodon dactylon*),
    72, 74
cough, 8
cowslip, water (*Caltha palustris*), 108
crab apple, Japanese flowering (*Malus
    floribunda*), 70
crimson passionflower (*Passiflora cinnabarina*),
    83
crinkle bush (*Lomatia silaifolia*), 118

lamb's tail (*Anredera cordifolia*), 105
larkspur (*Delphinium*), 53
laurel, Grecian (*Laurus nobilis*), 69
lavender, French (*Lavandula dentata*), 63
lawn, 72–76
  mowing, 124
lead, 23
lemon (*Citrus limon*), 68
lemon scented ironbark (*Eucalyptus staigeriana*), 115
leonurus cardiaca, 117
leopardbane (*Arnica montana*), 106
lettuce, prickly (*Lactuca serriola*), 117
lilac, Californian (*Ceanothus cyaneus*), 61
  perfume, 122
lillypilly (*Acmena centimetreena smithii, Syzyium*), 67
lime (*Citrus aurantiifolia*), 68
limestone fuchsia (*Eremophila freelingii*), 114
liquidambar (*Liquidambar styraciflua*), 96
lobelia, 54–55
lotus, 118
lymph nodes, 3
lymphocytes, 3

## M

macaw plant (*Daubentonia*), 112
macrophages, 3
Madeira vine (*Anredera cordifolia*), 105
magnolia (*Magnolia grandiflora*), 70
maidenhair tree (*Gingko biloba*), 69, 115
mango (*Mangifera indica*), 118
maple (*Acer*), 93
Marguerite daisy (*Chrysanthemum*), 110
marigold, marsh (*Caltha palustris*), 108
marigold, pot (*Calendula officinalis*), 100
marjoram (*Origanum marjorana*), 88
marmalade bush (*Streptosolen jamesonii*), 64
marsh marigold (*Caltha palustris*), 108
mazus pumilio, 79
meat, 132
medication
  preventive, 10–11, 17, 131
  relieving, 12–13
medick (*Medicago sativa*), 118
mentha diemenica, 79
metabisulphite, 131
Mexican poppy (*Argemone*), 106
mignonette vine (*Anredera cordifolia*), 105

milfoil (*Achillea millefolium*), 103
mint (*Mentha*), 88
monkshood (*Aconitum napellus*), 103
monosodium glutamate, 133
Monterey cypress (*Cupressus macrocarpa*), 95
moonflower (*Calonyction aculeatum*), 108
mould, 142
mountain devil (*Lambertia formosa*), 117
mountain tobacco (*Arnica montana*), 106
mouth breathing, 16
mowing, 124
MSG, 133
mucus, 8
mulberry (*Morus*), 96, 119
mulches, 127–129
mustard (*Brassica*), 107
myrtle, willow (*Agonis marginata*), 67

## N

nasturtium (*Tropaeolum*), 56
native grape (*Legnephora moorei*), 117
native plants, 58
  grasses, 72–73, 75
native violet (*Viola hederacea*), 80
nebuliser, 12
nemesia strumosa, 55
nightshade, jasmine (*Solanum jasminoides*), 85
Norfolk Island pine (*Araucaria heterophylla*), 67
nose, 6
  polyps, 18
  sprays, 17
nuts, 131

## O

oak (*Quercus*), 97
old man banksia (*Banksia serrata*), 68
old man's beard (*Clematis*), 110
oleander (*Merium oleander*), 119
olive (*Olea*), 96
onion (*Allium*), 104
onion, bog (*Arisaema*), 106
onionwood (*Dysoxylum*), 114
orange (*Citrus aurantium, C. sinensis*), 68
orange browallia (*Streptosolen jamesonii*), 64
orange locust (*Daubentonia*), 112
orchid tree (*Bauhinia acuminata*), 60
oregano (*Origanum vulgare*), 88
organic chemicals, 139

osage orange (*Maclura pomifera*), 118
ox-eye daisy (*Chrysanthemum*), 110

## P

paddy melon (*Cucumis*), 112
paints, 139
pansy (*Viola* x *wittrockiana*), 56
paperbark (*Melaleuca*), 70, 71
parsley (*Petroselinum crispum*), 88
pasque flower (*Pulsatilla vulgaris*), 51, 120
passionflower, crimson (*Passiflora cinnabarina*), 83
passionfruit (*Passiflora edulis*), 84
pasture grasses, 76
Paterson's curse (*Echium vulgare*), 99, 114
paving, 73, 128
paw paw (*Carica papaya*), 68, 109
peak flow meter, 134-135
pebble mulch, 128
pellitory (*Parietaria judaica*), 98-99
pencil cedar (*Dysoxylum*), 114
pennyroyal (*Mentha pulegium*), 88
pepper (*Capsicum*), 108
pepper leaf senna (*Cassia*), 109
peppermint gum (*Eucalyptus nicholii*), 69
peppermint tree, Western Australian (*Agonis flexuosa*), 67, 71
perfume (cosmetics), 139
perfume (plants), 122, 125
periwinkle, variegated (*Vinca major 'Variegata'*), 80
pest control, 126
pets, 138
petunia (*Petunia* x *hybrida*), 55
phlox, 55
pickled onion test, 132
pimpernel, scarlet (*Anagallis arvensis*), 104
pincushion plant (*Hakea laurina*), 62
pine (*Pinus*), 71
pine, Norfolk Island (*Araucaria heterophylla*), 67
pineapple (*Ananas comosus*), 104
pinebark mulch, 128
pipsissewa (*Chimaphila umbellata*), 110
plane tree (*Platanus* x *hybrida*), 97
plantain (*Plantago*), 30, 98
plantain, water (*Alisma plantago aquatica*), 103
plasma cells, 3
plumbago (*Plumbago auriculata*), 63

poet's jasmine (*Jasminium officinale*), 117
poinsettia (*Euphorbia pulcherrima*), 100
poison sage (*Isotropis*), 117
poison walnut (*Cryptocarya pleurasperma*), 111
pollen, 20-23, 30-48, 138
pollution, 23, 125, 139
polyanthus (*Primula*), 101
polyps, nasal, 18
poplar (*Populus deltoides*), 71, 97
poppy, celandine (*Chelidonium majus*), 110
pot marigold (*Calendula officinalis*), 100
pot plants, 142
potato vine (*Ipomoea batatas*), 116
potato vine (*Solanum jasminoides*), 85
power stations, 23
prednisone, 10
preventive medication, 10-11, 131
   sprays, 17
prickly lettuce (*Lactuca serriola*), 117
prickly paddy melon (*Cucumis*), 112
prickly pear (*Opuntia*), 119
primrose (*Primula*), 101
primula, 101
privet (*Ligustrum*), 30, 95, 118, 124
prunus, 71
puffers, 12, 13
pyrethrum-based pesticides, 126

## Q

Queensland itch tree (*Davidsonia pruriens*), 113
quick decay mulches, 128-129
quince (*Cydonia oblonga*), 112

## R

radiata pine (*Pinus radiata*), 71
Radio-Allergo-Sorbent Test, 25
ragweed (*Ambrosia artemisiifolia*), 99
rashes, 18-19
RAST test, 25
red bean (*Dysoxylum*), 114

red boronia (*Boronia heterophylla*), 60
red cedar, eastern (*Juniperus virginiana*), 117
red crumbweed (*Dysphania*), 114
red flowering paperbark (*Melaleuca hypericifolia*), 70
red mulberry (*Morus rubra*), 119
red root amaranth (*Amaranthus retroflexus*), 104
redbud (*Cercis canadensis*), 110
rhododendron, 64
rhus tree (*Toxicodendron succedaneum*), 101
rice grass (*Microlaena stipoides*), 74
Rio rosewood (*Dalbergia*), 112
river rose (*Bauera rubioides*), 59
rock poison (*Isotoma*), 116
rose (*Rosa*), 84
rose, guelder (*Viburnum opulus*), 65
rose, river (*Bauera rubioides*), 59
rosemary (*Rosmarinus officinalis*), 80, 89
rosemary, coastal (*Westringia fruticosa*), 65
rosewood, Rio (*Dalbergia*), 112
rosy heath myrtle (*Baeckia ramosissima*), 78
rough bearded grass (*Echinopogon*), 114
rubber vine (*Cryptostegia grandiflora*), 111
rye-grass (*Lolium perenne*), 76
    pollen, 22

## S

sage (*Salvia officinalis*), 89
sage, poison (*Isotropis*), 117
salbutamol, 12
sallee, black (*Eucalyptus stellulata*), 71
salt and pepper (*Agrimonia eupatoria*), 103
salvia, 64
sandbox tree (Hura crepitans), 116
sassafras, yellow (*Doryphora sassafras*), 113
savory, summer (*Satureja hortensis*), 89
scarlet pimpernel (*Anagallis arvensis*), 104
scribbly gum (*Eucalyptus haemostoma*), 69
seafood, 132
seasonal allergic rhinitis, *see* hayfever
senna (*Cassia*), 109
shasta daisy (*Chrysanthemum*), 110
she-oak (*Casuarina equisetifolia*), 94
shepherd's purse (*Capsella bursa-pastoris*), 108
shrubs
    allergenic, 93–98
    safe, 58–65
silky oak (*Grevillea robusta*), 69

silky tea tree (*Leptospermum lanigerum* v. *macrocarpum*), 63
silver-leaved plants, 80
sinusitis, 16
skin irritants, 102–122, 134
skin prick allergy test, 11, 25
slash pine (*Pinus elliotti*), 71
slow decay mulches, 128
smoke, 23
snapdragon (*Antirrhinum majus*), 51–52
sneezeweed (*Helenium*), 115
snow gum (*Eucalyptus pauciflora*), 71
snowball (*Viburnum opulus*), 65
snow-in-summer (*Cerastium tomentosum*), 78
South African daisy (*Dimorphotheca*), 113
spacer device, 12
spear grass, black (*Heteropogon contortus*), 116
spider plant (*Cleome*), 110
spiked aloe (*Agave*), 103
spinach, English (*Spinacia oleracea*), 57
spleen, 3
sprays, 17, 18
squirting cucumber (*Ecballium elaterium*), 114
star jasmine (*Trachelospermum jasminoides*), 85
steroids, 11
    sprays, 18
stinging tree (*Dendrocnide*), 113
stinkwort (*Inula graveolens*), 116
stress, 138
summer savory (*Satureja hortensis*), 89
sundew (*Drosera*), 113
sunglasses, 125
sunray (*Heliotropium*), 115
sweet Alice, 51
sweet bay (*Laurus nobilis*), 69
sweet corn, 57
sweet potato vine (*Ipomoea batatas*), 116
sweet William (*Dianthus barbatus*), 54
symptom diary chart, 26–27

## T

taro (*Calocasia esculentum*), 111
tarweed, yellow (*Amsinchia*), 104
tea tree (*Leptospermum*), 63, 79
terbutalin, 12
tests, 25
tetterberry (*Bryonia*), 107
thistle of Peru fig (*Argemone*), 106
thunderstorms, 140–141

thyme (*Thymus*), 80, 89
tickweed (*Cleome*), 110
Timothy grass (*Phleum pratense*), 76
toadflax (*Linaria vulgaris*), 54
tobacco, mountain (*Arnica montana*), 106
tobacco, wild (*Nicotiana*), 119
tomato, 57
tonsils, 3
touch-me-not (*Impatiens non-tangere*), 116
traveller's joy (*Clematis*), 110
tree of heaven (*Ailanthus altissima*), 103
trees
    allergenic, 93–98
    pollen, 30
    safe, 66–71
trefoil, burr (*Medicago sativa*), 118
triggers for asthma, 9, 11
trumpet flower, evening (*Gelsemium sempervirens*), 115
trumpet vine (*Campsis*), 82, 108
tupelo (*Nyssa sylvatica*), 70–71
turnip, Indian (*Arisaema*), 106
twiggy heath myrtle (*Baeckia virgata*), 59

U
urticaria, 19

V
variegated periwinkle (*Vinca major 'Variegata'*), 80
vegetables, 57, 132
veldt daisy (*Dimorphotheca*), 113
Ventolin puffers, 12, 13
verbena, 56
violet, native (*Viola hederacea*), 80
vitamin C, 139
volcanic eruptions, 23

W
wallaby grass (*Danthonia*), 112
walnut (*Juglans*), 95
walnut, poison (*Cryptocarya pleurasperma*), 111

washing (laundry), 125
water cowslip (*Caltha palustris*), 108
water plantain (*Alisma plantago aquatica*), 103
wattle (*Acacia*), 93
wattle, brush (*Albizia lophantha*), 94
waves, 23
weeds, 98–99, 124
weeping grass (*Microlaena stipoides*), 74
weigela (*Weigela florida*), 65
Western Australian peppermint (*Agonis flexuosa*), 71
wheeze, 8
white bryony (*Bryonia*), 107
white cedar (*Melia azedarach*), 96
white correa (*Correa alba*), 61
white heath (*Epacris impressa*), 62
white honeysuckle banksia (*Banksia integrifolia*), 67
white veldt daisy (*Dimorphotheca*), 113
wild cucumber (*Cucumis*), 112
wild ginger (*Asarum*), 106
wild lettuce (*Lactuca serriola*), 117
wild macaw plant (*Daubentonia*), 112
wild tobacco (*Nicotiana*), 119
willow (*Salix*), 97
willow myrtle (*Agonis marginata*), 67
wind, 138
windbreak, 71
windows, 138
wind-pollinated plants, 125
windy days, 125
wolfsbane (*Aconitum napellus*), 103
wonga wonga vine (*Pandorea pandorana*), 83
wood anemone (*Anemone nemorosa*), 105
wood dust, 139
woodchip mulch, 128
woolly burr (*Medicago sativa*), 118
woolly everlasting daisy (*Helichrysum blandowskianum*), 115
work environments, 139
wormwood (*Artemisia absinthium*), 98, 106
woundwort (*Achillea millefolium*), 103

Y
yarrow (*Achillea millefolium*), 103
yellow burweeds (*Amsinchia*), 104
yellow jessamine (*Gelsemium sempervirens*), 115
yellow sassafras (*Doryphora sassafras*), 113

*Also by Mark Ragg*

# Silent Night
A guide for snorers and their bedmates . . .
and anyone else within hearing
*Hodder & Stoughton*
ISBN 07336 0261 4

There is nothing new about snoring. People have laughed about it and cried about it for centuries. But, snoring has a social cost — snorers have to sleep in the spare room and are banned from staying at friends' houses. Recently, doctors have realised that snoring is not good for your health.

Nowadays, medical journals have gone past debating whether snoring does any harm, and they discuss how much harm snoring can do. *Silent Night* takes up that interest and turns it from debate in academic journals to practical information for the people who really need it — the snorers and their suffering mates.

This comprehensive book is divided into four sections:
- *Section One* looks at normal breathing, normal sleep, what snoring is and snoring and obstructive sleep apnoea.
- *Section Two* is fifty pages of questions and answers about snoring.
- *Section Three* discusses how to manage snoring – how you know if it is serious, tests for snoring, lifestyle changes and when doctors are needed.
- *Section Four* sets out where to go for help.